Eastern Front 1941

Hungarian Soldier
VERSUS
Soviet Soldier

Péter Mujzer

Illustrated by Steve Noon

OSPREY PUBLISHING
Bloomsbury Publishing Plc
Kemp House, Chawley Park, Cumnor Hill, Oxford OX2 9PH, UK
29 Earlsfort Terrace, Dublin 2, Ireland
1385 Broadway, 5th Floor, New York, NY 10018, USA
E-mail: info@ospreypublishing.com
www.ospreypublishing.com

OSPREY is a trademark of Osprey Publishing Ltd

First published in Great Britain in 2021

A catalogue record for this book is available from the British Library.

ISBN: PB 9781472845658; eBook 9781472845665;
ePDF 9781472845634; XML 9781472845641

21 22 23 24 25   10 9 8 7 6 5 4 3 2 1

Maps by www.bounford.com
Index by Rob Munro
Typeset by PDQ Digital Media Solutions, Bungay, UK
Printed and bound in India by Replika Press Private Ltd.

Osprey Publishing supports the Woodland Trust, the UK's leading
woodland conservation charity.

To find out more about our authors and books visit
www.ospreypublishing.com. Here you will find extracts, author
interviews, details of forthcoming events and the option to sign up for
our newsletter.

Acknowledgements

I would like to thank the following individuals for their kind support in
terms of information and photographs, without which this book might
not have been possible: Zoltán Babucs, Péter Illésfalvi, Zsolt Pálinkás,
Philippe Rio and Levente Gábor Saáry. Special thanks to Patrick Cloutier
for translating Russian sources and to my editor, Nick Reynolds.

Artist's note

Readers may care to note that the original paintings from which the
colour plates in this book were prepared are available for private sale.
All reproduction copyright whatsoever is retained by the publishers. All
enquiries should be addressed to:

www.steve-noon.co.uk

The publishers regret that they can enter into no correspondence upon
this matter.

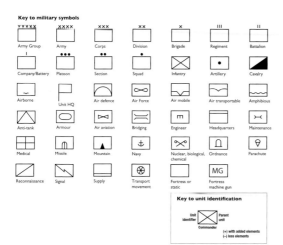

CONTENTS

Introduction

During the early hours of 22 June 1941, under the codename *Barbarossa*, Germany and its allies attacked the Soviet Union. At the outset, Hungarian involvement in this war was minimal. Hungary's society as well as its armed forces (Honvédség) were prepared to reconquer its lost territories of World War I from its neighbours. Suddenly this small country found itself in a total war, which in 1941 was remote, but in 1944–45 finally returned and crushed the Hungarian kingdom.

The Axis forces were divided into three army groups (*Heeresgruppen*); each had its own territorial objectives, but their principal aim was to trap and

The Red Army remained formidable despite being weakened by purges and hampered by reorganizations. These Soviet troops wearing SSh-39 steel helmets and M35 tunics pose with an M1910/30 Maxim medium machine gun, PPSh-41 submachine guns and M1891/30 rifles. (russiainphoto.ru/Sergey Korshunov/MAMM/MDF)

annihilate the Red Army (Krasnaya Armiya), preferably within 400–500km of the Soviet Union border. Our focus in this book is on Heeresgruppe Süd (Army Group South), commanded by Generalfeldmarschall Gerd von Rundstedt. His aim was to destroy the Soviet forces in Galicia (a region between Central and Eastern Europe) and Western Ukraine by means of a swift strike from the area of Lublin in central Poland to Kiev in north-central Ukraine, crossing the River Dnepr, and then advancing rapidly south-east along the river, in a single envelopment, preventing the escape of the units of the Red Army. Heeresgruppe Süd consisted of three armies (*Armeeoberkommandos*): AOK 6, AOK 17 and AOK 11 along the Soviet–Polish border north and west of Lvov in central Ukraine. Between AOK 17 and AOK 11 lay a gap running along the mountainous terrain of the Carpathian Mountains, belonging to Hungary. Of the three army groups, Heeresgruppe Süd had the highest number of non-German forces: 325,000 Romanian, 96,000 Hungarian, 62,000 Italian and 45,000 Slovakian troops.

The Soviet forces opposing the Hungarians were better prepared than the other Red Army units along the border. In the event of a German attack, Soviet planners expected the main weight of the Axis offensive to fall south of the Pripet Marshes. The Kiev Military District, under the leadership of Colonel-General Mikhail P. Kirponos, was responsible for manning the 940km-long line of defence. The Soviet troops were deployed in four armies, from north to south the 5th, 6th, 26th and 12th. The 12th Army was located on the Soviet–Hungarian border, from Borislav to Kamenets-Podol'skiy in western Ukraine. Upon mobilization the Kiev Military District became the Southwestern Front; it had 907,000 men under arms.

As far as terrain was concerned, there were significant river obstacles, especially the River Bug on the Polish border, the River Dnestr facing Romania, and the River Dnepr. The impassable Pripet Marshes also constituted an obstacle on the northern flank of Heeresgruppe Süd. The land was largely flat, except for the starting operational area of the Hungarian forces, which lay in the Carpathian Mountains. The road networks in the

ABOVE LEFT
Admiral Miklós Horthy, the Hungarian head of state, is escorted by his lifeguards into the reconquered town of Szatmárnémeti (modern-day Satu Mare, Romania), 5 September 1940. This photograph epitomizes Hungary's primary goal: retaking those territories lost after World War I. The lifeguards are armed with 35M rifles and 37M service pistols. (Authors' collection)

ABOVE RIGHT
Hungarian and Soviet officers at the border station at Lavochne, 22 March 1941. At a unique moment in Soviet–Hungarian relations, the Soviet Union handed back the Hungarian war flags captured by the Imperial Russian Army in 1848 in an effort to keep Hungary out of the impending war. (HM HIM 28490)

1 28 June 1941: Subordinated to Heeresgruppe Süd and tasked with the advance of AOK 17, Hungarian forces break out of the Carpathian Mountains and advance to the River Dnestr, reaching it on 9 July.

2 Early July 1941: Under continuous pressure from Axis forces, the units of the 18th and 12th armies withdraw alongside the River Prut.

3 8 August 1941: The 6th and 12th armies are forced to surrender at Uman.

4 10–16 August 1941: The Mobile Corps participates in the battle of Nikolayev (modern-day Mykolaiv, Ukraine).

5 30 August–6 October 1941: The Mobile Corps takes part in the Axis river defence at the Dnepr.

6 10 October 1941: The Mobile Corps begins to advance towards Izyum, reaching it on 28 October.

Carpathian Mountains were limited to only a few passable roads and railway lines going through valleys and passes. Otherwise the terrain was ideal for conducting mobile warfare in the event of dry weather, a mix of trees and bushes in the northern areas giving way to treeless plains and agricultural fields in the south. However, in the event of rainy weather in spring and autumn the soil turned to particularly nasty mud, which dried slowly. By European standards roads did not exist; the highways were few and at best had a cobblestone surface pocked with huge potholes. The railway gauges were different from the European standard, which further complicated the supply chain during the whole war.

At the end of World War I, Hungary was part of the Habsburg Monarchy, and ended up on the losing side. Owing to the peace conditions, Hungary was reduced from 282,000 to 93,000 square kilometres and the population from 18 million to 9.5 million. Hungary's leaders and people were determined to regain the territory lost in the wake of World War I and a close relationship with Germany seemed to provide the only opportunity for Hungary to achieve this. From November 1938 to April 1941, the Hungarians (with German and Italian support and approval) regained a significant part of their lost territory. In return Hungary strongly committed itself to the Axis.

At the start of Operation *Barbarossa*, however, the role Hungarian forces would play in the fighting was not clear to either side's planning staffs. The Soviet planners postulated a threat by Germany supported by Finland, Romania, Italy and possibly Hungary against the western Soviet Union and by Japan in East Asia. As a consequence of this, the Soviet government strove to make positive overtures to Hungary in an effort to keep the Hungarians out of the conflict for as long as possible. In early 1941, the Soviets handed back the war flags of the Hungarian Revolutionary Army of 1848–49 captured by the Russian Army. Even as late as 4 June, the Soviets secretly enquired about the Hungarian position in the event of a Soviet–German conflict and in return for Hungarian neutrality offered to support Hungary's further territorial demands against Romania.

When the Germans began preparing for the *Barbarossa* campaign, they did not intend to involve Hungary as a combatant in the war against the

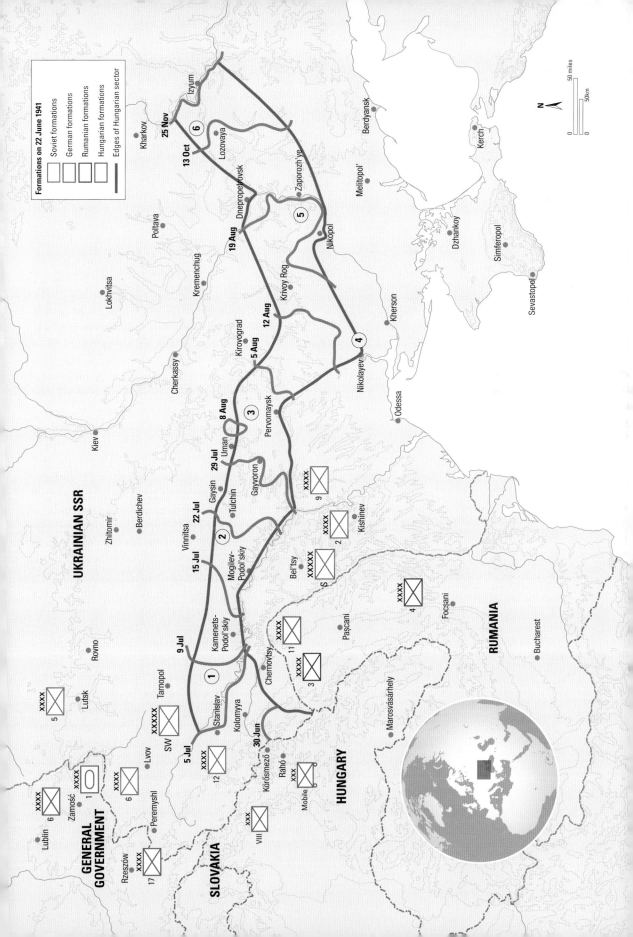

ABOVE LEFT
Marshal of the Soviet Union Semen M. Budennyi (right), commander of the Southwestern Direction (Southwestern and Southern fronts) from July to September 1941, inspects a horse-drawn supply unit with a young artillery lieutenant. (russiainphoto.ru/Ivan Shagin/MAMM/MDF)

ABOVE RIGHT
Major-General Béla Miklós, commander of the Mobile Corps, sits on a three-legged hunting stool accompanied by two of his staff officers. The officer at left has a non-regulation canvas pistol holster. (Fortepan/Varga Csaba dr.)

Soviet Union. Generaloberst Franz Halder, the chief-of-staff of the German Army's High Command (OKH, Oberkommando des Heeres), responsible for directing the opening stages of Operation *Barbarossa*, commented that it would be futile for the Germans to rely upon allies that were not entirely reliable, such as Hungary, noting that Hungary had no motive for fighting against the Soviet Union (Kamenir 2008: 4).

Even so, the Hungarian military leadership was unofficially kept informed by the Germans. At the military level, some kind of intelligence cooperation between the Hungarians and Germans clearly existed. From the spring of 1941, unmarked German spy aircraft took off from Hungarian airfields to fly covert missions over Soviet territory. Hungarian Junkers Ju 86 photo-reconnaissance aircraft also flew high-altitude sorties over the Carpathian Mountains at the behest of the Germans.

When war broke out between Germany and the Soviet Union, the Hungarians closed the Hungarian–Soviet border, activated the border-defence system and reinforced the border-guard and air-defence troops. While the Soviet 6th and 26th armies were heavily engaged from the beginning of the German onslaught, the 12th Army facing the Hungarian border reported no enemy activity on 23 June.

At 1240hrs on 26 June, Soviet Polikarpov I-16 fighters strafed an express train travelling from Kőrösmező (modern-day Yasinia, Ukraine) to Budapest, killing one civilian and wounding several others. Half an hour later, three unidentified aircraft – thought by many to have been Red Air Force Tupolev SB twin-engined bombers – attacked the Hungarian town of Kassa (modern-day Košice, Slovakia), killing 32 people and wounding more than 110. It was a perfect *casus belli* for Hungary's pro-German military leadership to involve the country in the war against the Soviet Union. The following morning the Royal Hungarian Air Force (MKHL, Magyar Királyi Honvéd Légierő) attacked Soviet targets in Ukraine; mobilization of the selected units was ordered and Hungary and the Soviet Union were at war.

The Opposing Sides

ORIGINS AND DOCTRINE

Soviet

By the mid-1930s, Marshal Mikhail N. Tukhachevskii had transformed the Red Army from a basic infantry and cavalry army into a formidable mechanized and armoured fighting force supported by airborne troops and a massive air force. In June 1941 the Red Army had 5,373,000 men under arms. It consisted of 198 rifle, 13 cavalry, 61 tank and 31 mechanized divisions, organized into 62 rifle corps, four cavalry corps, five airborne corps and 29 mechanized corps. Among the rifle divisions there were 19 mountain-rifle divisions, recruiting heavily from the Transcaucasian Military District.

Despite its imposing size, however, the Red Army was in serious disarray in June 1941. Its senior commanders attempted to implement a defensive strategy with operational concepts based on the offensive deep battles and deep operations theory while at the same time working to expand, reorganize, and re-equip its forces. The poor performance of the Soviet troops in Poland and Finland hung over the Red Army, and the widespread purges of the Soviet armed forces in 1938 effectively decapitated the officer corps, with many of the best and sharpest minds in the Red Army falling prey to Stalin's paranoia.

At the outbreak of war with Germany, the Southwestern Front contained the 5th, 6th, 26th and 12th armies along the frontier. The 16th and 19th armies were in reserve behind the forward forces. The Southern Front had the 9th Army and the Black Sea Fleet with its naval and naval aviation units. Deployed on the Soviet–Hungarian border, from Borislav to Kamenets-Podol'skiy, the 12th Army consisted of the 13th and 17th Rifle corps, the 16th Mechanized Corps and the 10th, 11th and 12th Fortified regions, plus artillery, engineering and other units. The 12th Army fielded six rifle divisions, five of them being mountain-rifle divisions, two tank divisions,

This artwork depicts a Soviet light-machine-gunner charging Hungarian positions on the island of Khortytsia on 2 September 1941. While this man is in his twenties, many of the soldiers of the 965th Rifle Regiment were reservists aged between 40 and 45.

Weapons, dress and equipment

The Soviet soldier is armed with a bipod-mounted 7.62mm DP light machine gun (**1**), the standard squad automatic weapon of the Red Army's infantry; it had a distinctive 47-round drum magazine.

His battered headgear is the SSh-39 steel helmet (**2**) with a circular liner. His field uniform consists of the M35 cotton field blouse (**3**), here with the 1940-pattern infantry collar tabs with infantry insignia (**4**). He also wears cotton M35 breeches (**5**) and M38 ankle boots with puttees (**6**).

His brown leather waist belt (**7**) supports a canvas Limonka F-1 grenade pouch (**8**) containing three F-1 fragmentation grenades at the left front, a water bottle in a canvas cover (**9**) at the rear and an entrenching tool in a canvas cover (**10**) at the right rear. He carries a DP ammunition pouch (**11**) containing spare drum magazines, slung over his right shoulder and resting behind his left hip.

one mechanized division, one motorcycle regiment, one artillery brigade and four artillery regiments; each fortified region was equivalent to a brigade. Only half of the Red Army infantry units faced the Hungarians, however, the other half being committed against German and Romanian forces. The 16th Mechanized Corps was located deep behind the first Soviet line.

Hungarian military intelligence calculated that the Soviet forces opposing them consisted of ten rifle divisions, one mountain-rifle division, two cavalry divisions and three mechanized divisions in the Hungarian–Soviet border area. This proved to be a major overestimate. The Soviet troops actually facing the Hungarians were the 58th and 192nd Mountain Rifle divisions of the 13th Rifle Corps, and the 96th Mountain Rifle Division of the 17th Rifle Corps.

Hungarian

During Hungary's secret rearmament, the Hungarian Army initially concentrated on enlarging its manpower and building up supplies of those armaments forbidden by the 1920 Treaty of Trianon. While the Hungarian Army was very traditional in its focus upon infantry supported by artillery, cavalry and support units, Hungary's senior military leadership also followed German, Italian and Soviet military theories concerning the development, organization and deployment of aviation and mechanized forces.

The fully mobilized strength of the Hungarian Army was 450,000 men. Owing to an extensive increase in manpower in May 1941, the Hungarian Army had nine corps organized under three army commands, plus the Mobile Corps, the Anti-Aircraft Artillery Corps, one aviation brigade and one River Forces brigade. The Hungarian order of battle consisted of 27 infantry, two border-guard, one mountain, two motorized rifle and two cavalry brigades. The artillery had 97 field-, six horsed, 28 motorized and 43 anti-aircraft artillery batteries. The Royal Hungarian Air Force had two fighter, two bomber and one short-range reconnaissance regiments, one long-range reconnaissance battalion and one paratrooper battalion. The units were on peacetime footings: the infantry brigades had just one infantry regiment

The pride of the Royal Hungarian Army: a hussar squadron parades in Budapest in front of the king of Italy, Victor Emmanuel III, in May 1937. The hussars had their old, traditional cavalry training upgraded with the use of new weapons and equipment. The cavalry was the most vulnerable part of the Mobile Corps, however, due to the sheer number of horses, which made supply and deployment difficult. (Fortepan/Bojár Sándor)

each, and in case of mobilization the existing units were duplicated using the resources of the already existing troops.

The Carpathian Operational Group organized to carry out operations against the Red Army consisted of VIII Corps and the Mobile Corps assisted by an aviation group and supporting troops. VIII Corps had the 1st Mountain Brigade, the 8th Border Guard Brigade and reinforcements. The 1st Mountain Brigade had four mountain-rifle battalions and one mountain-artillery battalion. The 8th Border Guard Brigade consisted of six border-guard battalions and one field-artillery battalion. VIII Corps was reinforced with two bicycle battalions, six anti-aircraft artillery battalions, one field- and one medium motorized artillery battalions, two engineer battalions and one railway-construction battalion.

The Mobile Corps was a complex formation, made-up of motorized rifle, bicycle and cavalry battalions. During the 1941 operations, the Mobile Corps deployed three out of four brigades: the 1st and 2nd Motorized Rifle and 1st Cavalry brigades (the 2nd Cavalry Brigade was left at home). The Mobile Corps was reinforced with three medium-artillery, two bicycle, one engineer and one signals battalions. The armoured element consisted of reconnaissance, bicycle/light-tank and armoured cavalry battalions. The artillery had motorized light-howitzer battalions, horse-drawn light-gun battalions and anti-aircraft batteries.

In June 1941 the Mobile Corps was equipped with 508 light machine guns, 168 machine guns, 52 anti-tank rifles, 40 light mortars, 12 medium (81mm) mortars, 80 anti-tank guns, 60 anti-aircraft guns (80mm and 40mm) and 90 field-artillery pieces. The armoured elements of the Mobile Corps had 87 38M Toldi light tanks, 48 39M Csaba armoured cars and 60 FIAT Ansaldo (Italian CV33) tankettes. In theory, the Mobile Corps could harness the different off-road capabilities of its different elements; but while this approach was ideal for Central Europe, it was to prove less effective in Ukraine.

The Mobile Corps received its mobilization order at its peacetime garrisons on 26 June. It was ordered to assemble by 29 June. Mobilization was very slow, however, and had not been completed at the time of moving out,

This artwork depicts a Hungarian light-machine-gunner of the IV Platoon, 1st Company, 5th Motorized Rifle Battalion, in action on the island of Khortytsia. He is moving to a new firing position during the counter-attack against infiltrating Soviet forces of the 965th Rifle Regiment.

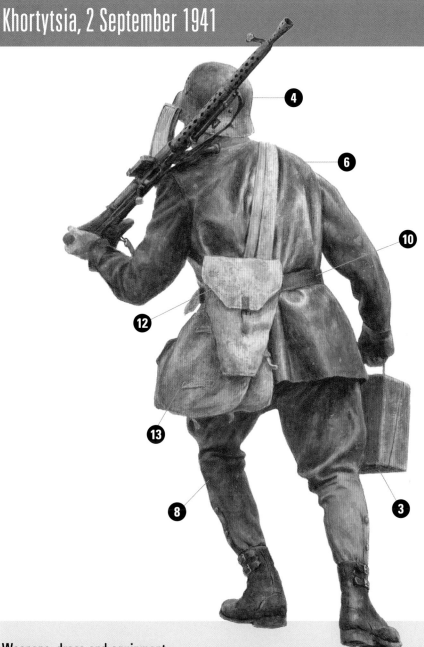

Weapons, dress and equipment

This soldier carries an 8mm 31M Solothurn light machine gun (**1**). This Swiss-designed weapon with a side-mounted 25-round curved box magazine produced a rate of fire of only 350rd/min. It fired from a bipod; the mounting system was upgraded in 1938 and every fourth gun received a tripod mounting, which allowed the 31M light machine gun to deliver more precise fire against ground and air targets. He also carries a 9mm 37M semi-automatic pistol (**2**) for self-defence, in a leather holster with two extra magazines. In his right-hand he carries a metal ammunition box (**3**), which contains five loaded magazines or loose rounds in paper boxes.

His headgear is the 35M steel helmet (**4**), almost identical to the German Stahlhelm 35. He wears a civilian flannel shirt under his field tunic with cornflower-blue collar tabs (**5**) denoting the Mobile Troops. His 30M leather jerkin (**6**), worn over his field tunic, was a popular and practical piece of uniform. The jerkin had woollen sleeves and no collar. His *Bocskai* field cap (**7**) is tucked into his belt. He wears 35M infantry trousers (**8**) and 35M marching boots (**9**) with two buckles and straps at the ankles.

His personal equipment includes the 20M leather service belt (**10**) with pistol holster, canvas magazine pouch (**11**), 34M Italian-style gas mask (**12**) and 35M bread bag (**13**), the latter containing his 35M canteen with cup, utensils and 34M mess tin.

its strength being only about 75–80 per cent. The units of VIII Corps were already alerted and assembled along the border to screen the Mobile Corps.

The aviation group supported the Hungarian ground forces with two fighter, one bomber and three short-range reconnaissance squadrons, equipped with 24 FIAT CR.42 fighters, 12 Junker Ju 86 bombers and 36 Heinkel He 46 and Weiss WM-21 short-range reconnaissance biplane aircraft. During the operations in Ukraine, Reggiane Re.2000 fighters and Caproni Ca.135 bombers also joined the aviation group.

RECRUITMENT, LOGISTICS AND MORALE

Soviet

The Red Army's manpower strength was based on conscription. The Soviet Union operated pre-conscription training for juveniles, consisting of physical training and indoctrination. Young Soviet citizens could join the OSOAVIAKhiM (Union of Societies of Assistance to Defence and Aviation-Chemical Construction of the USSR). This organization provided military training for Soviet youth, including driving of motor vehicles, shooting, parachuting, glider-flying and signalling. The organization claimed to have 13 million members in 1941.

The average Soviet conscript could have a very different background depending on his ethnicity, language, education, jobs and place of residence. Most were born as Russians, Ukrainians or Belarusians, but a significant proportion of the conscripts came from the Caucasian or Asian regions, some not even speaking or understanding Russian, the language of command in the Red Army. The treatment of conscripts was cruel by any standards.

The pre-emptive German attack on 22 June 1941 massively disrupted the Red Army's logistic network. The majority of the Soviet troops were already in staging and assembly areas grouped close to the border, or marching towards them. Mobilized civilians headed to the mobilization centres. Supply dumps had already been created along lines of communication to provide food, ammunition and fuel for the mobilized Army. German air raids and the rapid

Refuelling Soviet T-26 light tanks during an exercise in the late 1930s. Among the tanks are one twin-turreted T-26A M1931, three single-turreted T-26 M1933s, one T-26TU M1936 command tank and one ZIS-6-BZ fuel-tanker truck. (russiainphoto.ru/MAMM/MDF)

advance of German armoured and motorized troops interrupted, destroyed or captured the Soviet logistic lines, however. The ammunition issued to the Soviet troops was quickly exhausted by the intensity of operations, as were fuel and food stocks. The roads were soon littered with abandoned military vehicles and artillery pieces due to the shortage of fuel. Food supply was less problematic as it could be procured locally and the population at large was generally supportive of the Red Army.

The higher echelons were responsible for the medical evacuation of wounded combatants from the battlefield. In theory, two doctors operated at the battalion's aid station, while at platoon level one medic was available.

During the late 1930s and up to June 1941, Soviet citizens were subject to the so-called 'Great Terror', implemented by the Soviet state security authorities on the orders of Stalin. Political indoctrination was also a key issue in the Soviet armed forces. By the beginning of the *Barbarossa* campaign the attitude and morale of the individual Soviet soldiers varied greatly. Conscripts recruited from areas of Poland and the Baltic states that had been recently incorporated in the Soviet Union, as well as many Ukrainians, were less dedicated and motivated to fight for the Motherland. Once war came, even dedicated soldiers and officers were profoundly affected by the aggressive German onslaught. The constant Soviet withdrawals, the Luftwaffe's air superiority and the high-speed advance of the Axis armoured and mechanized forces combined in a deadly way with the questionable command skills of the young, inexperienced officers at every level of the Red Army's command structure, undermining its morale.

Soviet cavalry retained the horse-drawn machine-gun wagons carrying M1910/30 Maxim medium machine guns to provide mobile fire support to the cavalry. (russiainphoto.ru/ Victor Temin/MAMM/MDF)

Hungarian

The Hungarian armed forces were based on compulsory male military service since 1938. The compulsory pre-military *Levente* training targeted the physical fitness and the patriotic indoctrination of all Hungarian males from the age of 12 until they were conscripted. At the age of 21, later reduced to 19, men embarked on three years of military service before transferring to the reserve.

Owing to the recent addition of territories to Hungary, significant minorities (Slovakian, Ruthenian, Romanian and Yugoslavian) served in the Army. They were classified as less loyal members of the armed forces and were normally selected for non-combatant roles in the supply services or labour units. However, Slovakian and Ruthenian conscripts would also use their language skills to communicate with the local population, interrogate prisoners and carry out clandestine reconnaissance patrols in Ukraine.

The troops had their daily allotted ammunition calculated for different weapons, carried by the troops and the combat supply column. The rifles and light machine guns had two quantities of ammunition, one carried by the troopers and the other transported by the supply column, while medium machine guns had one quantity with the crew and three with the supply train. For example, the allotted ammunition for a soldier armed with an 8mm FÉG 35M bolt-action rifle was 80 rounds carried by the soldier and another 80 rounds stored with the company supply wagon. At brigade level, a further 80 rounds were stored.

Hungarian military cuisine was very traditional. The hot meals cooked at battalion and company level were prepared in two-wheeled field kitchens, called the 'goulash cannon'. Although the regulations stipulated that six days of food supply had to be kept with the battalion supply column, normally just one day's supply was held at battalion level. The troops also had emergency field rations consisting of bread and canned meats kept in their field packs. These could be eaten on order by the commanding officer.

Owing to the inadequate road network, logistical support for the advancing troops was difficult; sometimes fuel, food and ammunition had to be air-delivered to the troops via Savoia-Marchetti SM.75 transport aircraft. Vehicle maintenance measures were ineffectual; there was a lack of recovery vehicles and trailers and the mobilized civilian trucks were in poor condition. The troops often had to live by foraging, eating what they found, confiscated or captured from the enemy and taken from the local population. Ukraine was the so-called 'bread basket' of the Soviet Union with huge agricultural lands. In summertime there was plenty of fruit, vegetables, poultry and pigs to supplement the field rations. According to enlisted men's memories, after simply surviving the campaign in the East, the quantity and quality of the food was the second most important issue. Looting was a serious crime in the Hungarian Army as in others, but it was believed that the supply shortfall had

Hungarian motorized supply columns were equipped with military and mobilized civilian trucks still bearing the logos of their civilian owners. These Hungarian drivers, some wearing non-regulation items, pose with a German soldier. A significant part of the supply columns was equipped with civilian motor vehicles, horses and wagons, which were called up in case of mobilization. The movement-control units and the railway traffic coordination centre strove to deliver the troops by train as close as possible to the assembly areas. The narrow supply route in the Carpathian Mountains caused never-ending traffic jams, meaning that the supply column became separated from the troops and supplies could not be delivered on schedule. Based on a German–Hungarian logistic agreement, the Germans supplied the Hungarians with food, fuel and ammunition, as well as spare parts for German-origin vehicles and weapons in Hungarian service. Even so, the majority of the Hungarian resupply should have arrived from Hungary. (Author's collection)

Pictured on 23 July, these Hungarian motorized rifles are crossing the River Bug on a 38M Botond truck followed by a dispatch rider on a Puch G350 motorcycle. The river crossing has been built from a 33M aluminium bridge placed on pontoons. The main objective of the Hungarian troops was to keep up with the advancing German and Romanian forces, securing their flanks, following the retreating Red Army units and if possible capturing them. It is interesting to note, though, that the Soviet forces were always superior in numbers and weapons to the pursuing Hungarian forces. (NL-HaNA)

to be addressed. The quartermasters tried to formalize the on-the-spot supply measures by focusing on the use of captured and abandoned Soviet military and state-owned resources.

At battalion level, medical provision was provided by one junior reserve medical officer, one NCO, two orderlies and four stretcher-bearers. At company level, one medical NCO and four stretcher-bearers were available. The surgical instruments and procedures were outdated. According to the regulations, medical evacuation columns and field hospitals were organized at higher levels. During the first five days of the operation, however, VIII Corps had no medical provision; due to the slow mobilization, the 24th Medical Column only arrived on 30 June and required 1–2 days to reach operational readiness, a delay that had negative consequences for those with serious injuries.

Like the rest of Hungarian society, Hungarian Army soldiers were determined to fight for the territories lost after World War I. Hungary was governed by an anti-communist regime, but the Soviet Union seemed remote until the outbreak of World War II. Traditionally, Hungarian society viewed the Russian Empire and then the Soviet Union as a hostile but distant European power. The Hungarians did not forget or forgive the Russian support for crushing their revolt against the Habsburg Monarchy in 1848–49, or the destruction caused by the Imperial Russian Army on Hungarian soil in 1914. The short-lived Soviet-style Hungarian communist regime in 1919 also left a bitter taste, especially among the middle and upper classes. The situation changed drastically in September–October 1939 when Poland collapsed under the combined attack of the German and Soviet forces, and Hungary and the Soviet Union suddenly became neighbours.

In 1941, the war against the Soviet Union was not a life-or-death matter for Hungarian soldiers, NCOs and officers, or for Hungarian society in general. It was viewed more like an unavoidable sacrifice that had to be made in exchange for the recovery of lost territories – especially if the sacrifice was made by somebody else. The enlisted men just wanted to survive the deployment and to return to civilian life as soon as possible. The commissioned officers and NCOs were mostly motivated by their professional attitudes; the war was a necessary element of their careers, and represented an opportunity to be decorated and promoted. The memory of World War I had not faded; the senior officers had already served as juniors in that conflict and a significant part of the junior officers' corps were orphans inspired by the heroism of their fallen fathers.

Although many among the enlisted men did not see why Hungary should fight the Soviet Union, the deployed units of the Mobile Corps (hussars, bicycle, motorized rifles and armoured troops) and the mountain-rifle and border-guard units were elite troops, many of whom had taken part in the Hungarian Army's operations since 1938. The troops and the officers knew and trusted each other. The good or excellent operational achievements of the troops were based mostly on the troops' loyalty to their units and leaders rather than upon their determination to fight and defeat Soviet soldiers.

WEAPONS, TRAINING AND TACTICS

Soviet

Soviet infantry weapons were known for their simplicity, ruggedness and reliability. The standard rifle of the Red Army was the 7.62mm Mosin-Nagant M1891/30 bolt-action rifle and from about 1937 onwards the M1891/30 sniping rifle was issued with a telescopic sight known as the PU. In 1938 the 7.62mm M38 carbine was also introduced. The Red Army was the first to adopt semi-automatic rifles on a large scale, namely the 7.62mm Tokarev SVT-38 and SVT-40, with a ten-round detachable box magazine. These self-loading rifles were issued mainly to NCOs and could be equipped with telescopic sights for snipers. Soviet infantry squads were armed with the bipod-mounted 7.62mm Degtyaryov DP light machine gun with its distinctive 47-round drum magazine. The Soviet infantry used F-1, RGD-33 fragmentation and RPG-40 anti-tank grenades and the so-called 'Molotov cocktails'. They also employed PMD-series anti-personnel mines and dog mines, intended to be used against armoured vehicles.

The Red Army was armed with the 7.62mm Maxim M1910 medium machine gun, firing from a 250-round fabric cartridge belt at 520–600rd/min. The Red Army also relied heavily on mortars of different calibres, these being issued to the troops in large quantities. Company-level mortars were the 50mm 50-BM-38, -39, -40 and -41 light mortars. The 82mm 82-BM-36, -37 and -41 medium mortars were identical to the 81mm French Brandt mortar

These Soviet anti-tank rifle teams are armed with the single-shot 14.5mm PTRD-41 anti-tank rifle, a simple but deadly weapon when used against the Hungarian light armoured vehicles. The PTRD-41 was rushed into service in July 1941. It was a fairly effective close-range anti-tank weapon against lighter armoured vehicles, and could penetrate any deployed Hungarian armoured vehicle. The semi-automatic 14.5mm PTRS-41 anti-tank rifle entered service within a few months of the PTRD-41. (russiainphoto.ru/Arkady Shaikhet)

A Soviet 76.2mm M1927 regimental gun in an open firing position. Its high-explosive fragmentation rounds proved very successful against soft targets. The crew wear the SSh-39 steel helmet; the gun commander has leather binocular and map cases. (russiainphoto.ru/Victor Temin/MAMM/MDF)

except for the increased calibre. The 107mm 107-BM-38, an enlarged version of the 82mm mortar, was produced especially for the Red Army's mountain infantry. The BM-38 could be broken down for pack-animal transport, or it could be attached to a two wheeled horse-drawn limber. The 120mm 120-HM-38 heavy mortar was also an enlarged version of the 82-BM-37.

In 1941 the Red Army used the 45mm M1932 and M1937 anti-tank guns which fired 1.43kg APHE, APCR, HE and canister rounds. The guns' rate of fire was 15–20rd/min and the armour penetration was 43mm at 500m and 35mm at 1,000m. At divisional level the strength of the Soviet artillery was reduced significantly before the outbreak of war, with the divisional artillery regiment having just 16 76.2mm field guns and eight 122mm field howitzers. The anti-aircraft artillery employed 7.62mm Tokarev 4M M1931 four-barrelled machine guns, 12.7mm DShK heavy machine guns and 37mm M1939 (61-K) light automatic air-defence guns. The medium anti-aircraft artillery had 76.2mm M1931 (3-K9) and 85mm M1939 (52-K) air-defence guns.

Red Army infantry tactics were simplistic and straightforward, reflecting the inexperience of its officers and soldiers. The tactics focused on small-unit movement and battle formations and the layout of defensive positions. This system proved to be rigid and unable to adapt to quickly changing tactical situations. Weapons training was also restricted due to shortages of ammunition and actual weapons – many soldiers fired just 3–5 rounds with their rifle during training – and even officers and NCOs had difficulty mastering their weapons' complexities during their hasty training. Most soldiers had to learn soldierly conduct and weapons handling while fighting with their units on the battlefield.

According to Hungarian intelligence reports and the questioning of prisoners of war, the Hungarians faced a wide spectrum of Red Army units: border guards, ordinary rifles, mountain rifles, cavalry and mechanized forces. In theory, Soviet mountain troops were kitted out with appropriate uniforms and climbing gear and trained to be able to operate in highlands far more effectively than conventional infantry. This was not the case in 1941, however. German intelligence reports based on prisoner-of-war interrogations noted that many captured troops of the 20th Mountain Rifle Division (3rd Rifle Corps, Transcaucasian Military District) were in their late thirties or older – too old for mountain warfare, in the view of their captors – and lacked formal mountain-warfare training; their division differed from standard rifle divisions only in the greater number of mules and horses in its supply units (Zaloga & Ness 1998: 45–46).

Despite the obvious shortcomings of Red Army training, the Hungarians found their Soviet opponents to be flexible, stubborn and determined.

Firing a 40kg shell, the Soviet 152mm M1909/30 horse-drawn howitzer with wooden spoked wheels was still in service in 1941. (russiainphoto.ru/Victor Temin/MAMM/MDF)

In general terms the Red Army carried out an organized retreat, using delaying actions and counter-strikes to unbalance the pursuing Hungarian troops. The Soviets developed their methods based on the element of surprise, overwhelming firepower, skilful use of camouflage and, last but not least, local knowledge and the support of the civilian population – but this was not the case everywhere. Given sufficient time and resources, Soviet forces laid ambushes in chosen locations, and let Hungarian reconnaissance patrols and vanguards cross the Soviet lines. When the main forces of an advancing Hungarian motorized rifle battalion reached the killing zone, the Soviets opened up with mortars and automatic weapons from the flanks and rear, trapping the surprised and shocked Hungarians. It took time for the Hungarians to take cover and to deploy their heavy weapons, requesting support from artillery or armoured forces.

In case of ambushes, the Soviet troops utilized their infantry firepower based on numerous automatic weapons, such as submachine guns, self-loading rifles and machine guns. According to Hungarian reports, the Soviets also used explosive and white-phosphorous ammunition, resulting in severe injuries to Hungarian troops. Snipers were an integral part of Red Army rifle and mounted units; their dedicated role was to target enemy officers, heavy-weapons crews and signalmen. Hungarian officers and NCOs were easy targets for Soviet snipers as they wore prominent insignia and polished riding boots and carried binoculars and map cases.

A significant proportion of the ordinary Soviet soldiers were determined to fight, were prepared to act alone, and fought until the very end. The Hungarians were surprised that in hopeless situations the Soviet soldiers did not surrender. Almost from the beginning of hostilities it was not easy for the Hungarians to identify who was a soldier and who belonged to the local population. During this period many thousands of Soviet soldiers and a significant number of conscript-aged male civilians were hiding, wandering about or escaping behind enemy lines. Most of them wanted to re-join the Red Army. Also, the military situation was very fluid in Ukraine, as the Axis mechanized units deeply penetrated the Soviet defence. Infantry units followed on behind, to take over and pacify the conquered territories. Between them lay a no-man's-land in which soldiers, deserters and partisans could appear out of the blue and attack

Axis supply columns. In some cases the Soviets wore Hungarian uniforms, taken from casualties or prisoners of war, to entrap their Axis opponents. From the beginning of the campaign Hungarian troops reported that their missing colleagues were often found executed, their bodies having been mutilated by Soviet soldiers. Obviously, capturing armed Soviet soldiers wearing Hungarian uniform or civilian clothing had fatal consequences.

Hungarian

As well as the officers and NCOs, Hungarian support and supply personnel were also armed with service pistols for self-defence, due to a lack of rifles. The 9mm 29M and 37M semi-automatic pistols, produced by FÉG, were simple and robust blow-back weapons, serviceable and reliable. Chambered for a 9mm round, both pistols had a seven-round detachable box magazine.

At the beginning of the *Barbarossa* campaign the Hungarian Army was equipped with 8mm 31M and 35M Mannlicher service rifles and carbines. In 1941, the deployed units of the Mobile Corps had no submachine guns. Only the paratroopers and the assault engineers were armed with German 9mm 35M Bergmann submachine guns in 1941. The standard squad automatic weapon was the 8mm 31M Solothurn light machine gun. The standard Hungarian medium machine gun was the 8mm 07/31M Schwarzlose, re-barrelled to fire the new 31M cartridge. The Hungarians used home-produced 31M and 36M Vécsey hand grenades and the 38/AM flame grenade.

The rifle companies' heavy-weapons platoons each had two light mortars and two anti-tank rifles. The Hungarian troops also had the domestically designed 50mm 39M light mortar. The battalion-level medium mortar was the 81mm 36M.

The Hungarians adopted the German 37mm PaK 36 anti-tank gun as the 36M. The artillery of the Mobile Corps consisted of horsed and motorized artillery; the troops of VIII Corps used horsed, motorized artillery and pack-transported mountain guns too.

A Hungarian infantry squad dressed in field blouses and *bocskai* field caps clean their 35M rifles and 31M light machine guns. The Hungarian Army retained the 8×50mmR cartridge and the straight-pull 95M Mannlicher rifle until it adopted a new 8×56mmR cartridge in 1931, along with the 31M rifle. The original 95M rifles were re-barrelled in large quantities to take the new cartridge. The Hungarians also developed their own turn-bolt service rifle based on the Mannlicher design to fire their 31M rimmed cartridge. This development resulted in the 35M, the best Mannlicher rifle, which used the protruding Mannlicher clip-loaded five-round magazine. According to some photographic evidence the 35M rifle had a sniping version, but Hungarian troops never received telescopic-sighted rifles for sniping in 1941. (Fortepan/Kókány Jenő)

The horsed artillery battalions were equipped with 80mm 18M light field guns, while the motorized artillery battalions had 105mm 37M light howitzers (the German leFH 18) towed by 37M Hansa-Lloyd half-tracked artillery tractors. The corps-level artillery deployed motorized medium howitzer battalions equipped with 150mm howitzers towed by elderly Italian Pavesi artillery tractors. The anti-aircraft artillery battalions had 80mm 29M guns and 40mm 36M Bofors autocannon towed by Pavesi tractors and Ford Marmon trucks.

The speed of the Hungarian mobile troops provided the military leadership with an excellent opportunity to deploy selected units to a given point on the battlefield in a short time to engage the enemy. Training in the Mobile Corps was centred on the means of transportation for the troops. As Hungary was a predominantly agricultural country, handling and riding horses was not too difficult for the village boys, whereas cycling was much more demanding. Operating motor vehicles, trucks and armoured vehicles needed more-educated men with skills and training. Hungarian Jews were usually among the most educated part of Hungarian society and so were most likely to have a driving licence, be a mechanic or possess other important skills, but in 1941 Hungarian Jews were not permitted to serve with the combat troops.

The motorized rifle battalions were converted from the light-infantry battalions and grenadier companies, and constituted a kind of elite light-infantry force. Their tactical skills were based on a more independent, flexible mission-oriented training. In the bicycle battalions the training focused on long-range cycling exercises with full kit for the bicycle troops.

Given their organization and equipment, the armoured troops were really only suited for reconnaissance and liaison duties. At best, the tankettes in use were mobile machine-gun platforms to support the infantry. Although the light tanks and armoured cars were able to conduct reconnaissance, in battle they would be deployed against superior forces, including dug-in anti-tank guns and artillery positions, and would suffer severe losses as a result.

Under the new organization introduced on 18 February 1941, the Hungarian Army's motorized rifle brigades had one light-tank battalion and one reconnaissance battalion, and the cavalry brigade had one armoured cavalry battalion. The 1st Motorized Rifle Brigade had the 9th Bicycle/Light Tank Battalion while the 2nd Motorized Rifle Brigade had the 11th Bicycle/Light Tank Battalion. The battalions' title and organization reflected their transitional status, existing bicycle battalions having been converted to light-tank battalions. Each bicycle/light-tank battalion was meant to consist of the battalion headquarters (three 38M Toldi light tanks), sapper, signals and maintenance platoons and the 1st and 2nd Bicycle companies and 3rd and 4th Light Tank companies (each with 18 38M Toldi light tanks).

Hungarian troops with a 20mm 36M anti-tank rifle. This weapon's armour penetration was only 15–18mm at a range of 300m, and the rate of fire was 30–35rd/min, making it severely outdated by 1941. The loader is posing with his 37M service pistol behind the metal ammunition box of the anti-tank rifle. (Author's collection)

This Hungarian mortar team is pictured on exercises with a 36M mortar, the best battalion-level heavy weapon available to the Hungarian troops. Transported in three parts, this weapon entered service in 1936; it was subsequently modified as the 36/39M mortar. The troops wear 17M and 35M steel helmets and are armed only with service pistols. (Author's collection)

During the 1941 operations the staff of the Mobile Corps developed a method to pursue the enemy. In theory the two motorized rifle brigades were deployed on different, parallel roads and the cavalry brigade was deployed between them. The brigade commanders created different combat groups – a system previously employed during the short Yugoslavian Campaign of April 1941 – to fulfil the allotted tasks. Each of these so-called combat groups was named after its commander, who was normally the senior battalion commander or a staff officer from brigade headquarters. The combat groups each consisted of one or two motorized rifle battalions and one bicycle battalion, reinforced with one or two light-howitzer batteries, sappers and a light-tank platoon or company. The brigade anti-aircraft batteries each had six

The backbone of the Hungarian armoured troops: the 38M Toldi light tank. This example carries two different unit insignia: the white lightning bolt of the 1st Reconnaissance Battalion and the white Turul bird of the 1st Armoured Cavalry Battalion. (Fortepan/Divéky István)

36M Bofors autocannon – used against air and ground targets – which were allocated in pairs or singly to support the combat groups. This practice did mean, however, that the brigade commanders could find that their resources were depleted, making it hard to reinforce their troops when it really counted.

The forward echelon of a motorized rifle brigade consisted of the reconnaissance battalion, which was reinforced by light-tank, anti-aircraft, sapper, anti-tank, machine-gun and traffic-control platoons, one light-howitzer battery and one motorized rifle company.

The commander's objective in case of contact was to outflank the enemy or overrun him frontally with deployed troops supported by the brigade artillery. According to regulations, the motorized rifles were transported in their trucks until they were close to the combat zone, at which point they were meant to leave their trucks behind and make their final approach on foot. It was a similar course of action for the cavalry and bicycle troops, who were to leave behind their horses, bicycles and vehicles. Only the reconnaissance and tank troops went into action in their armoured vehicles, trucks and motorcycles, reconnaissance troops dismounting when contact was made with the enemy.

In some cases the Hungarians neglected reconnaissance and ran into Soviet ambushes or counter-attacks. On the other hand, some Hungarian units used covert reconnaissance parties of soldiers with Slovakian or Ruthenian backgrounds, armed but wearing civilian clothes, to explore the enemy lines.

COMMAND, CONTROL AND COMMUNICATIONS

Soviet

The 12th Army was subordinated to the Kiev Military District, under the leadership of Colonel-General Kirponos. The 12th Army's commander, Major-General Pavel G. Ponedelin, was a veteran of World War I; during the Russian Civil War (1917–22), he commanded a regiment and then a brigade. In 1940, he was chief-of-staff of the Leningrad Military District, becoming commander of the 12th Army in March 1941.

The 13th Rifle Corps was commanded by Major-General Nikolai K. Kirillov, who had served in staff and command position before the war, commanding

Soviet officers conduct shooting practice with assorted pistols, from left: P 08, Tokarev TT-33 and Mosin-Nagant M1895 revolver. The officers and NCOs were armed with pistols and revolvers, with many platoon and company commanders also carrying submachine guns. The standard service pistols were the Tokarev TT-30 and TT-33, based on the Colt-Browning M1911 design, chambered to fire the 7.62mm M30 pistol cartridge and using a detachable eight-round box magazine. Some officers and NCOs were armed with the 7.62mm Nagant M1895 revolver, a pre-World War I design; it had a seven-round cylinder. (russiainphoto.ru/ MAMM/MDF)

Based on the US Ford V8-40, the Soviet GAZ M-1 command car was produced from 1936 to 1941. A 1st lieutenant of the Tank Troops stands next to the car, wearing an M35 tunic and a service cap. Note the snow chains attached to the car's rear tyre, an attempt to aid traction in muddy terrain. (Philippe Rio)

the 19th Rifle Division before taking over command of his corps in 1938. The 58th Mountain Rifle Division was commanded by Major-General Nikolai I. Proshkin, a Russian Civil War veteran who had graduated from the Frunze Military Academy in 1938. According to a staff inspection, Proshkin's division was considered to be the least capable in the 12th Army in terms of morale and training (Maslov 2001: 13). Proshkin worked hard to improve his division's combat readiness. The 192nd Mountain Rifle Division was commanded by Major-General Petr F. Privalov, who had been deputy commander of an infantry division before taking command of his division in 1939.

The 17th Rifle Corps was commanded by Major-General Ivan V. Galanin. A graduate of the Frunze Military Academy, he commanded the 57th Rifle Division during the battles of Khalkhin Gol in May–September 1939; and after leading his corps in the battle of Uman in July–August 1941 and the subsequent retreat east through Ukraine, he took command of the 12th Army on 25 August 1941. The 96th Mountain Rifle Division, the Soviet formation most frequently encountered by the Hungarian troops, was commanded by Colonel Ivan M. Shepetov. Shepetov joined the Red Army in 1918, graduated from the Infantry and Cavalry School and, in 1934, from the Frunze Military Academy.

The Red Army operated a dual-command system inherited from the Russian Civil War, in which the communist leaders did not trust the former Tsarist officers who led the Red Army. The commissars, officially called political officers, functioned at each level from battalion up to the highest echelon. The commissar had to give his approval for any major order by the unit commander, but many commissars used their position to intervene in military matters and intimidate unit commanders and officers. Although the dual-command system ended in August 1940, commissars remained with the troops (Bellamy 2007: 86).

The widespread purges of the Soviet Armed Forces in 1938 decapitated the officer corps. As a consequence, in early 1941 the Red Army accelerated its officer training programmes by doubling the numbers of military schools and increasing graduate numbers. In early 1941, there was still a shortfall of 80,000 officers, however, and 12.4 per cent of senior and regimental commanders lacked any formal military education (Glantz 2005: 468).

The Red Army's junior officers undertook a three-year course at a military college, but this period was reduced to 4–10 months shortly before the outbreak of war. Reserve officers were called up in huge numbers. As so many of the Red Army's senior leadership had 'disappeared' during the purges, a young platoon commander could rapidly find himself commanding a battalion without any formal training for the task.

In 1941, Red Army signals units were equipped with insufficient quantities of what were largely obsolete domestically produced radios. Battalions had their signals platoons, while regiments had signals companies and divisions had signals battalions. The signals platoon had a seven-man radio group with four RRU sets (7–8km range) and one 6-PKA set (20–30km range) and three wire/optical squads equipped with signal lamps and field telephones, each squad having a cart. In Soviet armoured units only the company commanders' vehicles had radios; the rest communicated by means of signal flags.

Red Army communications were severely degraded at the beginning of the *Barbarossa* campaign, due to acts of sabotage conducted by German special forces, effective air raids conducted by the Luftwaffe and the fluid operational situation. As a result, the Soviet higher command was forced to operate in an information vacuum in which radio communication did not work and telephone lines were interrupted. The Soviet higher command echelons had to despatch liaison officers to try to get a clear picture of what was happening, while unit commanders became reluctant to use their radios and relied heavily on telephone communication and runners.

Hungarian

The senior commanders of the Hungarian Army had served in the Austro-Hungarian Army before and during World War I. The Carpathian Operational Group was directly subordinated to the chief-of-staff, Colonel-General Henrik Werth, and led by the commander of VIII Corps, Lieutenant-General Ferenc Szombathelyi, a former commander of the Ludovika Military Academy (1936–38). The Mobile Corps was commanded by Major-General Béla Miklós, a cavalry officer. The commander of the 1st Motorized Rifle Brigade since 1940 was Major-General Jenő Major, a veteran of the elite 11th Field Jäger Battalion during World War I. The 2nd Motorized Rifle Brigade was led by Major-General János Vörös, an artillery officer, while the 1st Cavalry Brigade was commanded by Major-General Antal Vattay, a cavalry officer and former *aide-de-camp* to Admiral Miklós Horthy, the regent of Hungary.

The Hungarian Army battalion commanders had also been trained before and during World War I, and experienced that conflict as junior officers. They had commanded their battalions since 1938–39, but were mostly former cavalry or bicycle-troop officers with limited knowledge of mechanized warfare. Professional soldiers commanding companies and platoons had been thoroughly trained at the Ludovika Military Academy in Budapest; the four-year curriculum was demanding and provided practical and theoretical instruction. Many troop and platoon commanders were reserve officers, however, who had undertaken regimental reserve officer candidate courses instead.

Hungarian Army units fought under German command and Hungarian liaison teams were assigned to Heeresgruppe Süd, AOK 11 and AOK 17 and to Luftflotte 4. The Hungarian liaison officers often found it hard to reconcile German demands with the Hungarians' fighting capacity.

As with the Red Army, battlefield communications during mobile warfare proved to be a major issue for the Hungarians. Although the landlines worked between the rear echelon and the corps and brigade headquarters, communications with the fighting troops depended upon unreliable radio sets, dispatch riders and liaison officers. At battalion level, each unit had a signals platoon mainly equipped with Hungarian-made radio sets. The R/1 and R/2 sets (400–1,600m range) with arch antenna were used by the companies to communicate within their battalion network. These radios were transported to the front line by trucks or mules and in combat were carried on the radio operator's back. The R/3 sets (up to 15km range) were used by the artillery to communicate with friendly troops. Each battalion had a signals truck equipped with an R/7 radio set (30km range), which allowed the battalion commander and his staff to communicate with their subordinates and the brigade or corps headquarters. Hungarian armoured cars and light tanks had their own radio sets but the tankettes had no radio equipment at all, instead using hand and flag signals. The mountainous terrain, the summer storms and the high concentration of ores in the terrain could also negatively influence the radios' range and signal quality.

Opening Battles

4–13 July 1941

BACKGROUND TO BATTLE

On 25 June, before Hungary entered the fighting, NKVD border guards approached their Hungarian opposite numbers and initiated a conversation, asking about Hungarian intentions related to the unfolding Axis invasion of the Soviet Union. After a seemingly friendly chat the Soviets withdrew; the Hungarians reported the incident through the chain of command.

Between AOK 17 and AOK 11 lay a gap running along the terrain of the Carpathian Mountains screened by the Hungarian border-defence forces. The successful German operation at Lvov (22–30 June) meant that the Hungarians would have to move quickly to keep up with the advancing German forces.

Armed with a DP light machine gun and Mosin-Nagant rifles with fixed bayonets, these Soviet infantry in a makeshift position are covering their retreating units. (russiainphoto.ru/Victor Temin/MAMM/MDF)

Troops of the 9th Bicycle/ Light Tank Battalion are rail-transported towards the assembly area. The 38M Toldi light tanks are on flat cars; between the tanks is a 31M light machine gun on an anti-aircraft tripod. The 9th Bicycle/Light Tank Battalion was mobilized on 27 June, with the recalled reservists required to report to their units by 29 June. The battalion headquarters with its subordinated sapper and signals platoons and the two light-tank companies with 20 officers and 424 men embarked at Jászberény railway station on 1 July. The 9th Bicycle/Light Tank Battalion reached Rahó (modern-day Rakhiv, Ukraine) on 3 July, unloaded and started to march towards the front line on 4 July. The heavy rains made the advance of the battalion's vehicles difficult in the muddy conditions. Several trucks fell into the River Prut; it took a lot of work to recover them. (Zoltán Babucs)

The task of the Hungarian forces was to maintain the connection between AOK 17, the Romanian Third Army and AOK 11 and to pursue the withdrawing Red Army units.

The first goal of the Carpathian Operational Group was to capture the Zaleshchiki–Kolomyya–Stanislav area. The units of VIII Corps were tasked to clear the passes of the north-eastern Carpathian Mountains and capture the towns of Deliatyn, Nadvornaya, Dolina and Skole in the highlands. After that, the Mobile Corps could be deployed along the cleared mountain roads and passes to advance into the region lying south of the River Dnestr, southern Galicia. Then, the deployed Hungarian motorized rifles, cavalry and bicycle troops supported by light tanks and artillery would pursue the withdrawing Soviet forces and aim to capture the intact bridges to keep the Axis advance moving.

The 12th Army, without even experiencing much pressure from the Hungarians, also retreated east by order of the Front Command. With the Soviet forces rapidly evacuating the Kamenets-Podol'skiy Fortified Region, defensive works were destroyed, artillery pieces blown up, and all remaining weapons and property hastily removed. The rearguard forces of the 12th Army, which departed from the border to a new line during 2100–2200hrs on 27 June, noted the crossing of the Soviet border by units of the Hungarian military, which began to move in the direction of Osmoloda and Vishkov (Runov 2010: 146).

The Soviet border-guard and mountain-rifle troops, fighting in regiment-sized infantry groups reinforced with artillery and mortars, put up a fierce resistance. The upper Prut Valley was blocked by deep and wide mine belts. The only route available to the advancing Mobile Corps, the Körösmező–Tatarov–Deliatyn road, was severely damaged by blowing up bridges, railway lines and even culverts up to 40–50km inside Soviet territory. The withdrawing Soviet troops created obstacles for the advancing Hungarian troops by blowing up bridges wherever they could. Within the Carpathian Mountains, Soviet engineers destroyed 21 bridges and tunnels, and the rivers in flood also complicated the operations. Not all of the bridges were properly demolished, however; sometimes just one part of a bridge was blown up, which meant they were easier to rebuild. Beyond the town of Deliatyn, the Soviet engineers refrained from demolishing the bridges and roads.

Long-range reconnaissance aircraft of the Royal Hungarian Air Force reported that the retreat of the Soviet forces escalated from the region; the roads and railway lines were packed with troops and vehicles or waiting for embarkation around the railway stations. During 1–2 July the Hungarians began to move through the Carpathian mountain passes, chasing the units of the 58th Mountain Rifle Division (Southwestern Front) withdrawing from the border and fighting for the passes. On 2 July, Hungarian reconnaissance aircraft observed that the majority of the Soviet troops crossing the River Dnestr belonged to the 96th Mountain Rifle Division.

The advance of the Mobile Corps towards Kolomyya placed the entire right (north-eastern) flank of the 18th Army under threat of attack. Evaluating the situation, Lieutenant-General Andrei K. Smirnov, the 18th Army commander, ordered the commander of the 96th Mountain Rifle Division, Colonel Shepetov, to withdraw units to the northern bank of the River Siret and take up a defensive posture in the Beregomet–Glubokaya sector. The 58th and 96th Mountain Rifle divisions were not on a war footing when the operation started. Nominally, they were mountain units, but lacked sufficient pack-animal supply columns; moreover, their manpower and weaponry complements were not complete and they were deficient in terms of the specialized mountain training. A significant part of their transport capacity was to be provided by the mobilized civilian sector, but this never appeared.

At the time of the German invasion, the 60th Mountain Rifle Division was located in the foothills of the Carpathian Mountains near the border with Hungary as part of the 17th Rifle Corps. While the division was not attacked by the main German forces in the first days, its almost total lack of trucks and shortage of horses made it difficult to retreat to the east. The division had just 8,000 men, but was well provided for in terms of weapons: 7,742 bolt-action rifles and carbines, 349 semi-automatic rifles, 939 submachine guns, 357 light machine guns, 209 medium and heavy machine guns, eight 45mm anti-tank guns, 32 76mm cannon and howitzers, 24 122mm howitzers and 120 mortars. Owing to the lack of pack animals, carts and motor vehicles, however, most of the heavy weapons would be lost during the retreat. The 60th Mountain Rifle Division was soon transferred with 17th Rifle Corps to the new 18th Army (Southern Front), but returned to the 12th Army in mid-July.

The advancing Hungarian troops were able to take only 10km in four days; even their motor vehicles were more of a hindrance than a help. The mountain rifles captured the heavily defended town of Tatarov in the north-east foothills of the Carpathian Mountains on 2 July.

The first phase of the operation was dominated by the Hungarian mountain and border-guard troops, which slowly opened up the passes and repaired the destroyed bridges. Their activities enabled the Mobile Corps to cross the Carpathian Mountains following the 1st Mountain Brigade and start pursuing the withdrawing Soviet forces.

In June–July 1941 the breakthrough by Axis units in the Yarmolintsi region threatened the Kamenets-Podol'skiy Fortified Region and divisions of the 17th Rifle Corps, with a thrust from the north and rear. From the west, units of the Hungarian Mobile Corps advanced along the northern bank of the River Dnestr, toward Kamenets-Podol'skiy. The 18th and 12th armies withdrew alongside the River Prut. As the Hungarians had predicted, the Soviet troops performed an organized retreat, demolishing bridges and mining the roads and key positions. Shepetov deployed his 651st and 155th Mountain Rifle regiments to secure and cover the bridge over the River Prut at Chernovtsy to aid the escape of the withdrawing Red Army units as they retreated in the face of pressure from Romanian and German forces.

After initial difficulties, the Mobile Corps started its advance into the Stanislav plains, spearheaded by the 2nd Motorized Rifle Brigade, which took Deliatyn on 2 July; the town was captured by troops of the 6th Motorized Rifle Battalion approaching on foot. The battalion headed towards Kolomyya, annihilated a 150-strong Soviet rearguard and took the town. The local population welcomed the Hungarian troops with garlands. The friendly attitude was due to the NKVD's brutal massacre of prominent or hostile members of the local population. The Mobile Corps occupied Kolomyya, establishing communications with the right-flank (north-western) units of AOK 17, to which it was subordinated on 17 July. This reinforcement created a threat to the right (north-eastern) flank of the Southern Front.

Hungarian 38M Toldi light tanks of the 9th Bicycle/Light Tank Battalion pictured on their way to Kolomyya. Some of the light tanks still bear the old unit marking, the Turul bird, of the 1st Armoured Cavalry Battalion. Beneath the trees are 38M Botond trucks, concealed from Red Air Force air strikes. As of 1 July 1941, the 9th Bicycle/Light Tank Battalion's equipment consisted of 39 38M Toldi light tanks, 52 trucks, 11 cars, 39 motorcycles (two with sidecars), two ambulances, one signals truck and one fuel truck; the bicycle companies had 206 bicycles each. As the 9th Bicycle/Light Tank Battalion had a significant deficit in terms of motor vehicles the 1st Motorized Rifle Brigade's commander, Major-General Major, ordered Colonel Vilmos Néray, the battalion commander, to reassign the motor vehicles from the bicycle companies to the battalion staff and the two light-tank companies. (NL-HaNA)

MAP KEY

1 **1140hrs, 4 July:** The Hungarian Army's reinforced 2nd Company, 5th Motorized Rifle Battalion departs for Horodenka, the main force following it at 1200hrs.

2 *c.***1300hrs, 4 July:** The Hungarian advance guard comes under concentrated fire from two Red Army rifle battalions of the 96th Mountain Rifle Division at Horodenka. The motorized rifles storm the village.

3 **5 July:** Battle Group Benda (composed of the 4th and 5th Motorized Rifle battalions and the 12th Bicycle Battalion) attempts to capture the bridge over the River Dnestr at Zaleshchiki intact.

4 **Morning, 5 July:** The 6th Motorized Rifle Battalion captures Kitsman and clashes with elements of the 28th Cavalry Division coming from Chernovtsy.

5 **Night of 5/6 July:** The 6th Motorized Rifle Battalion holds its position, reinforced by an armoured-car platoon and one motorized rifle company from the 4th Motorized Rifle Battalion and support from the Royal Hungarian Air Force, until the Soviet troops withdraw from the area.

6 **6 July:** Owing to Hungarian pressure, the regiment-sized Red Army rifle units fighting stubbornly at the line of Kiselev–Zaleshchiki start to withdraw over the last intact bridge over the River Dnestr. The bridge is blown up by the Soviet sappers.

7 **13 July:** A Hungarian composite light-tank company of the 9th Bicycle/Light Tank Battalion, subordinate to Battle Group Püchler (Infanterie-Regiment 228, 101. leichte Infanterie-Division), is tasked with advancing through Minkovtsy and Antonovka and capturing Height 306, south of the village of Filyanovka.

8 **1630hrs, 13 July:** Hungarian 38M Toldi light tanks cross a creek at Minkovtsy, reaching and capturing Antonovka at 1700hrs and advancing to Novaya Ushitsa.

9 **After 1700hrs, 13 July:** On the north side of the road a contingent of Soviet infantry of about company strength, armed with machine guns, is hiding in the field. The Hungarians engage with two Soviet anti-tank guns located at Height 306.

10 **1730hrs, 13 July:** The composite light-tank company's I Platoon takes Height 306, capturing a third Soviet anti-tank gun.

11 **1800hrs, 13 July:** The I Platoon reaches the edge of the village of Filyanovka at twilight; camouflaged Soviet 45mm anti-tank guns knock out two Hungarian tanks.

12 **1815hrs, 13 July:** The company commander's tank and the tank of one of the Hungarian platoon commanders go forward. Soviet anti-tank guns knock out both tanks at a range of 200–300m.

13 *c.***1900hrs, 13 July:** The rest of the composite light-tank company deploy and outflank the village; two further 38M Toldi light tanks are destroyed. The remaining Toldi light tanks take up position west of Filyanovka.

Battlefield environment

In July 1941 the weather was warm, but rainy. The road system was largely destroyed by the Soviet forces or washed away by the rainfall. The rivers and creeks were flooded, making it difficult to build military bridges. The landscape featured low hills 300–400m high; it was covered with scrub and woodland and crossed by rivers and creeks. Visibility was generally good from early dawn through to evening, although somewhat obscured by early-morning fog in the valleys and river beds.

This Soviet sniper is armed with an M1891/30 rifle with PU telescopic sight and wears a hooded camouflaged overall. Next to him is his spotter with binoculars. Soviet snipers were tasked with targeting enemy officers, heavy-weapons crews and signalmen. (russiainphoto.ru/ Ivan Shagin/MAMM/MDF)

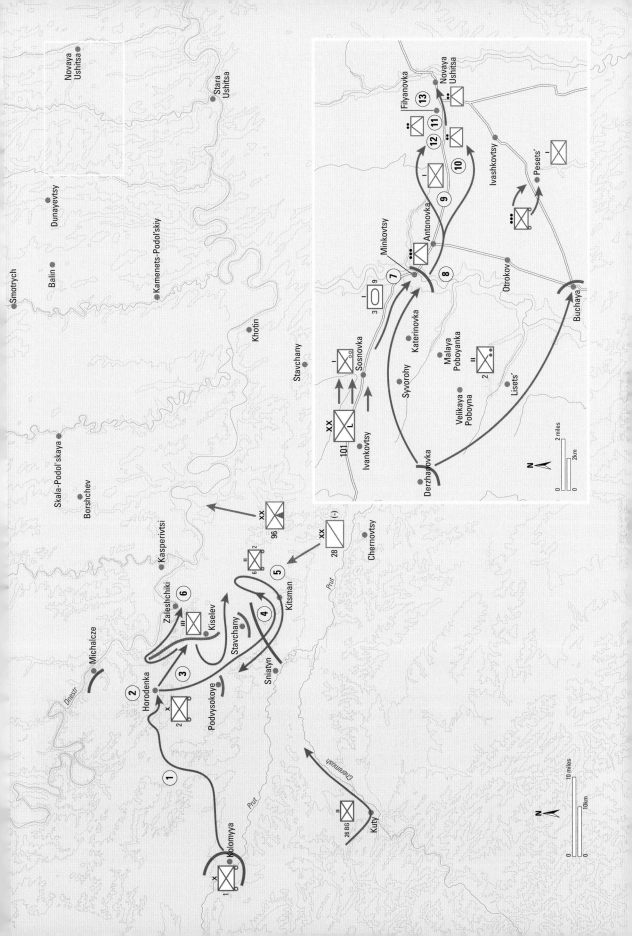

INTO COMBAT

The commander of the 2nd Motorized Rifle Brigade, Major-General János Vörös, was informed that only three bridges over the River Dnestr remained intact, two of them situated at Zaleshchiki. Vörös ordered the 5th Motorized Rifle Battalion, supported by the 4th Battery, 2nd Light Howitzer Battalion, to advance through Kolomyya to Horodenka on 4 July. Lieutenant-Colonel Lőrinc Latorczay, the commander of the 5th Motorized Rifle Battalion, placed his 2nd Company in the vanguard and ordered it to capture the bridge at Zaleshchiki and establish a bridgehead at Michalcze. The 2nd Company, commanded by Captain Frigyes Füszfás, was reinforced with three sapper squads, one machine-gun platoon and two 36M anti-tank guns. The 4th Battery, equipped with 37M light howitzers, was positioned between Füszfás' contingent and the remainder of Latorczay's battalion. The forward echelon departed at 1140hrs, the main force following it at 1200hrs.

The 5th Motorized Rifle Battalion advanced quickly; the vanguard passed through Kolomyya at 1245hrs and approached Horodenka. At about 1300hrs, the Hungarians came under concentrated fire from the Soviet rearguard, equivalent to about two infantry battalions. After spotting the quickly advancing Hungarians, the Soviet troops occupied their defensive positions and opened up on the attackers with automatic weapons and mortars. The Soviet troops fought desperately, seeking to buy time for their comrades to reach those bridges over the River Dnestr that were still intact.

Füszfás deployed his motorized rifles with the support of his Schwarzlose medium machine guns and anti-tank guns to destroy the Soviet units. The advance-guard troops broke into Horodenka and fought for every single house. Latorczay aided Füszfás' efforts by sending his 3rd Company to outflank the stubbornly resisting Soviet forces; the soldiers of the battalion headquarters were also deployed to overcome the defenders. The Soviet troops were pushed out of the village towards Serafin. Killed by a shot to the head, Füszfás was decorated with the Officer's Cross of the Hungarian Order of Merit.

On 5 July Vörös organized a battle group from the 4th and 5th Motorized Rifle and 12th Bicycle battalions; it was commanded by Colonel Antal Benda,

who had participated in the brief Hungarian campaign in Yugoslavia earlier in the year. Benda's task was to capture the bridge over the River Dnestr at Zaleshchiki intact. During the late afternoon of 5 July, Battle Group Benda deployed into combat between Horodenka and Serafin. By that time only one bridge remained intact over the Dnestr. The Hungarian motorized rifles and bicycle troops clashed with small Soviet units while approaching the Dnestr. The onset of darkness ended the advance and the Hungarians went into well-guarded bivouac positions near Horodenka.

The 5th Motorized Rifle Battalion's advance was slowed by stubborn Soviet resistance and Lieutenant-Colonel István Sándor's 4th Motorized Rifle Battalion was deployed to overcome the Soviet troops. Among the motorized rifles was Sergeant Lajos Pásztor, a 29-year-old professional NCO, commanding a rifle platoon of the 4th Motorized Rifle Battalion. According to Pásztor's citation, his platoon stopped a Soviet charge at Horodenka by outflanking and capturing a whole Red Army rifle company along with its weaponry. Owing to the combined effort of the soldiers of the 4th and 5th Motorized Rifle battalions the Soviets were pushed back further, to the village of Dzvynyach.

Supported from high ground nearby by the 2nd Company, 4th Motorized Rifle Battalion, one company of the 5th Motorized Rifle Battalion outflanked Dzvynyach from the south; the Hungarians stormed the village and the Soviet troops started to withdraw over the last intact bridge to the other side of the Dnestr. The bridge was blown up by the Soviet sappers, but Captain Dezső Dorner and a handful of his men from the 1st Rifle Company, 4th Motorized Rifle Battalion, crossed the river on the wreckage of the bridge, although Sándor believed this was impracticable. Dorner's party was separated from the Hungarian main force, but on 7 July captured an intact bridge at Kasperivtsi over the River Siret. Dorner achieved these feats without sustaining any casualties.

Meanwhile, Lieutenant-Colonel Zoltán Keményfy's 6th Motorized Rifle Battalion advanced towards Chernovtsy on 4 July. The lead element of the 6th Motorized Rifle Battalion was a half-company of motorized rifles riding on their 38M Botond all-terrain squad-carrier trucks followed by a light battery of 37M light howitzers towed by 37M Hansa-Lloyd half-tracked artillery

Clash at Horodenka

Soviet view: The scene depicts the situation near the village of Horodenka at about 1300hrs on 4 July, when the Soviet covering force taking up ambush positions opened fire on Hungarian trucks. In July 1941, the weather was warm and rainy, the vegetation was green and the visibility was good. The Soviet soldiers took up position on a commanding height on the western edge of the village. The NCO commanding this group is armed with a PPD-40 submachine gun. Wearing minimal equipment, the riflemen have the M1891/30 bolt-action rifle with *Schtyk* spike bayonet. The sniper aims his M1891/30 equipped with a PE telescopic sight, while the machine-gunner delivers covering fire with his DP light machine gun. From the village, 82-BM-36 mortar teams deliver interdiction fire on the Hungarian vehicles.

Hungarian view: The 5th Motorized Rifle Battalion was ordered to advance through Kolomyya to Horodenka. In the van, the 2nd Rifle Company was ambushed by Soviet rearguards at the entrance to the village. The Hungarians hastily disembark, taking cover behind their 38M Botond and Krupp-Protze trucks and shooting back. The young platoon commander, an ensign, has been shot and wounded by a Soviet sniper. The Krupp-Protze half-squad carrier truck with mounted 8mm 31M light machine gun provides immediate covering fire for the motorized riflemen. The Hungarian troops wear their normal combat kit and weapons; their backpacks have been left on the trucks. The ensign wears his distinctive officer's uniform, making him an ideal target for the snipers. At right, a truck driver wears the Italian-style 37M crash helmet.

tractors. The vanguard was closely followed by Keményfy's main force. It was getting dark when the Hungarian motorized rifles encountered some Soviet troops in front of the village of Sniatyn. When Keményfy ordered his troops to charge the village, the Soviet troops misidentified the 38M Botond trucks as enemy tanks and withdrew.

The 6th Motorized Rifle Battalion captured Kitsman, a major road intersection, during the morning of 5 July. The battalion's 3rd Company was in the town when its reconnaissance patrol reported Soviet trucks coming from Chernovtsy. The 50-strong Soviet contingent belonged to the 28th Cavalry Division. The Hungarian company commander deployed his motorized rifles outside of the town at the road intersection, but they soon found themselves under attack by a battalion-sized Soviet force. The Red Army units wanted to reach the far side of the Dnestr. After making contact with the Hungarians, the Soviet force kept getting bigger and stronger as more and more withdrawing troops joined it, and it soon outmatched the Hungarians in terms of manpower and armament.

Keményfy ordered his battalion to repel the attacking Soviet forces. Although the advance collapsed and the Soviet troops started to withdraw, the Red Army units soon renewed their attack. When Keményfy reported his status to brigade headquarters, he was ordered to maintain his position and wait for reinforcements, which consisted of an armoured-car platoon equipped with 39M Csaba armoured cars and one company from the 4th Motorized Rifle Battalion. Royal Hungarian Air Force He 46 aircraft of the VII Short-Range Reconnaissance Squadron strafed and bombed the Soviet troops with 10kg anti-personnel bombs. In the event, the 6th Motorized Rifle Battalion was able to hold its position until nightfall, when the Soviet troops withdrew from the area. Keményfy's battalion lost 12 men killed in action.

Although Hungarian reports identified the opposing Red Army cavalry formation as the 28th Cavalry Division, which moved from Chernovtsy, no Soviet sources place this division in the area at that time. While the 12th Army had no subordinated cavalry, the 6th Army had the 3rd and 14th Cavalry divisions. Soviet forces lost 200 men killed and 600 taken prisoner during the battles around Horodenka and Zaleshchiki.

As the Hungarian troops of the Carpathian Operational Group moved into flatter terrain, mobility became a key issue for the advancing Hungarian Army units. The troops of VIII Corps, the less mobile part of the Carpathian Operational Group, were assigned to mop up the areas that were already occupied and secure the Axis lines of communication, as well as the standard occupational security duties. At this point VIII Corps had 1,516 officers, 44,482 men, 12,861 horses, 2,032 horse-drawn carriages and 1,334 motor vehicles under command.

On 6 July the 9th Bicycle/Light Tank Battalion entered Kolomyya and was welcomed with flowers by the local Polish population. The Polish civilians looked upon the entering Hungarian troops as liberators; at least the Hungarians protected them from armed groups of Ukrainians. The 1st and 2nd Bicycle companies and the Maintenance Platoon caught up with the battalion on 8 July. On that day, Major formed an advanced reconnaissance team composed of the 1st Reconnaissance Battalion, 2nd Lieutenant László Simon's I Platoon of the 3rd Company, 9th Bicycle/Light Tank Battalion, and

Hungarian 36M Bofors anti-aircraft autocannon could also be used against ground targets. On 11 July, the 9th Bicycle/Light Tank Battalion's main vehicle column was attacked by three Red Air Force fighters near Smotrich; the Hungarian anti-aircraft gunners shot down all three aircraft. The troops of the 1st Motorized Rifle Brigade and the 9th Bicycle/Light Tank Battalion reached Dunayevtsy and camped inside the village. A second air strike hit the Hungarian troops in the village. According to Simon's memoirs, three I-16 fighters strafed the village, killing a Hungarian dispatch rider; this time the Hungarian anti-aircraft gunners shot down one of the aircraft (Babucs 2006: 24). (NL-HaNA)

two 36M Bofors autocannon and ordered it to explore the roads towards the River Zbruch and secure the bridges.

From 9 July, the Mobile Corps was subordinated to Heeresgruppe Süd, and was assigned to Panzergruppe 1. On that day, the 9th Bicycle/Light Tank Battalion crossed the River Dnestr in pouring rain; the roads were in a poor condition, the bridges had been blown up and the emergency/military bridges had been washed away by the flooding rivers.

The Soviet commander, Colonel-General Kirponos, ordered his 6th Army, reinforced with the 16th and 15th Mechanized corps, to hold firmly south of Berdichev, to protect the north-eastern wing of the Southwestern Front. Hungarian aerial reconnaissance revealed that the troops of the 17th Rifle Corps (18th Army) were retreating ahead of the Mobile Corps. The weather aided the Soviet troops, the pouring rain transforming the roads into impassable terrain. On 10 July, the troops of the 2nd Motorized Rifle Brigade captured Kamenets-Podol'skiy; the 1st Motorized Rifle Brigade advanced towards the Smotrich–Landskrone–Balin line.

On the afternoon of 12 July, two platoons of the 3rd Light Tank Company and one platoon of the 4th Light Tank Company were subordinated to a battle group led by Oberst Carl Püchler, commander of Infanterie-Regiment 228 (101. leichte Infanterie-Division). The three Hungarian Army light-tank platoons were led by Captain Tibor Kárpáthy, an experienced armoured-company commander who had graduated from the Ludovika Military Academy in 1926 as an infantry officer. He had commanded the Tankette Company of the 2nd Reconnaissance Battalion in 1939 during the operation in Carpathian Ruthenia and was decorated for his actions. During the Yugoslavian Campaign he commanded a light-tank company.

At about 1300hrs on 13 July, as the Hungarian tank crews enjoyed a rare hot meal on their light tanks, Püchler briefed Kárpáthy about the current tactical situation. Kárpáthy was ordered to advance through Minkovtsy and Antonovka and capture Height 306, south of the village of Filyanovka. As well as the three Hungarian Army light-tank platoons, the advancing forces consisted of one German bicycle company and two German anti-tank platoons with 37mm guns, with a German artillery battalion providing fire support. Based on the German intelligence estimate, just 5–6 Soviet machine-gun posts plus covering infantry were in position north of the road. This was not the case, however; the 17th Rifle Corps (60th and 96th Mountain Rifle and 164th Rifle divisions) left behind blocking detachments armed with 45mm anti-tank guns, covered by rifle companies and machine-gun teams. The anti-tank guns were positioned and camouflaged alongside the road connecting Antonovka and Filyanovka on the commanding Height 306, as well as at the edge of Filyanovka. Worn down by the constant retreat since the beginning of the fighting, the Soviet units' combat readiness depended on their NCOs and officers.

The 38M Toldi light tanks crossed a creek at Minkovtsy at 1630hrs and reached Antonovka at 1700hrs. Kárpáthy deployed his two anti-tank platoons alongside the road and the tank platoons flanking the village on both sides. The defenders were surprised by the quickly deployed Hungarian light tanks and anti-tank guns firing into the village. The demoralized Soviet troops were surrounded and the Hungarian and German troops captured 200 prisoners of war as well as a number of heavy weapons.

The Germans expected only sporadic and light resistance, so they urged Kárpáthy's force to press on and capture Novaya Ushitsa. According to the Germans, just a few enemy machine guns lay between the Hungarians' current position and this objective. The Hungarian tanks accelerated, leaving the German bicycle company behind. Anticipating light resistance, the leading light-tank platoon, 2nd Lieutenant Alfonz Dorsan's I Platoon, moved along the road followed by the company staff with Kárpáthy and the other two light-tank platoons. Roughly one company of Soviet infantry armed with machine guns were hiding in the field on the north side of the road.

The company staff and Candidate Sergeant Péter Hábel's II Platoon deployed to attack. At first they aimed southwards, leaving the road and intending to turn towards Height 306. Lacking radio contact with the other Hungarian tankers, 2nd Lieutenant Imre Kömlődy's III Platoon prepared for an attack on the north side of the road. Kömlődy's platoon advanced parallel with the road and engaged with two Soviet anti-tank weapons positioned at Height 306. The Soviet anti-tank gunners could not hit the quickly moving 38M Toldi light tanks and Kömlődy's platoon quickly captured the enemy anti-tank guns. Surprised by the Hungarian tanks' mobility, some of the Soviet anti-tank gunners abandoned their anti-tank guns and withdrew.

Dorsan's I Platoon assaulted Height 306 north of the road and captured a third Soviet anti-tank gun. At this point just one 38M Toldi light tank had been damaged and there were no Hungarian casualties. Kárpáthy and his company staff's tanks also reached Height 306. The leading light-tank platoon, Kömlődy's, identified new targets north of the road and Kárpáthy sent back one of his light tanks to Püchler with a report.

At 1730hrs, the Axis advance continued; the Soviet forces fired upon the Hungarian tanks from the nearby forest south of the road. At 1800hrs, Kárpáthy and two light-tank platoons turned off the main road on to a dirt road leading south. The field was littered with knocked-out and blown-up Soviet tanks and trucks. The leading light-tank platoon, Dorsan's, reached the edge of the village of Filyanovka at twilight (about 1815hrs), but Dorsan and his crew did not realize that camouflaged Soviet 45mm anti-tank guns were present; determined to fight back, these Soviet anti-tank gunners knocked out both Hungarian tanks. Dorsan was wounded in the leg and his two crewmen were killed. As he had no radio communication, Dorsan could not report the danger to his comrades.

Captain Tibor Kárpáthy, commander of the 3rd Light Tank Company of the 9th Bicycle/Light Tank Battalion, wearing mess dress. In the 9th Bicycle/Light Tank Battalion, the 1st Bicycle Company was commanded by Captain Károly Szabó, while Captain Jenő Farkas-Sági led the 2nd Bicycle Company and Captain Zoltán Barthalos led the 4th Light Tank Company. The two bicycle companies were deployed separately from the light tanks. Kárpáthy's battalion commander, Colonel Vilmos Néray, had fought during World War I as a junior infantry officer; Néray spent three years in Russian prisoner-of-war camps and probably learned Russian during that time. (Zoltán Babucs)

The scene after the battle at Filyanovka on 13 July, with captured Red Army weapons, dead Hungarian crewmen and a knocked-out Hungarian tank. Owing to the thinness of the 38M Toldi's armour, the Soviet 45mm armour-piercing shells did not detonate inside the vehicles; instead, they passed straight through the tanks, killing or wounding the crew. Even the Soviet anti-tank rifles could penetrate the 38M Toldi and the 39M Csaba armoured cars; and the Ansaldo tankettes were vulnerable to infantry fire too. (HM HIM 95522)

Kárpáthy saw that his leading tanks had stopped at the edge of the village. Owing to the lack of radio connection he decided to move forward to investigate, accompanied by Hábel's tank. At a range of 200–300m the Soviet anti-tank guns knocked out the company commander's tank. The driver and gunner were killed and Kárpáthy was seriously wounded; unable to leave his tank he lay helpless, waiting for the next shot. At that moment Hábel rushed in and halted his tank between the enemy and the damaged tank, thus protecting his company commander. The next shot hit Hábel's tank and all of its crew were killed. The rest of Kárpáthy's tanks moved into action, outflanking the village; a further two 38M Toldi light tanks were destroyed. The Soviet anti-tank gunners remained in their positions. The surviving 38M Toldi light tanks went in position west of Filyanovka. Kömlődy took over command from the wounded Kárpáthy, who was evacuated from the battlefield. The German troops only reached the Hungarian positions at 1950hrs.

During the action, Kárpáthy's force suffered gruelling casualties: six 38M Toldi light tanks were knocked out and nine crewmen were killed, eight of them due to the impact of the Soviet armour-piercing shells. In the event, the knocked-out tanks were repairable. The Soviet troops involved suffered 40–50 men killed in action; 8–10 machine guns and five anti-tank guns were captured and one tank was knocked out. During the night, while the Hungarians withdrew, leaving behind the knocked-out tanks and their deceased crewmen, Soviet reconnaissance parties moved across the battlefield, collecting information on the enemy. A report from Southern Front headquarters claimed that 13 Axis tanks were destroyed on 14 July (*sic*), and noted that Hungarian documents were found on the dead crewmen (Irinarkhov 2012: 321).

Major complained to the commander of 101. leichte Infanterie-Division, Generalleutnant Josef Brauner von Haydringen, because the Hungarian light tanks had been used for breaking through the enemy lines – a task beyond their capabilities. On 23 July, units of the Mobile Corps reached the River Bug and accomplished its first operational objective.

Golovanevsk

6 August 1941

BACKGROUND TO BATTLE

The battle of Uman (15 July–8 August 1941) was the Axis offensive operation against Lieutenant-General Ivan N. Muzychenko's 6th Army and Major-General Ponedelin's 12th Army. In the vicinity of Uman the German forces encircled two Soviet armies, about 25 divisions. The battle occurred during the Kiev defensive operation between the elements of the Red Army's Southwestern Front, retreating from the Lvov salient, and Heeresgruppe Süd, commanded by Generalfeldmarschall Gerd von Rundstedt. The Soviet forces were under overall command of the Southwestern Direction, commanded by Marshal Semen M. Budennyi, which included the Southwestern Front, commanded by Colonel-General Kirponos, and the Southern Front, commanded by General of the Army Ivan V. Tyulenev.

By the end of July, after crossing the River Bug, the Hungarian Army's Mobile Corps reached the Stalin Line at Golovanevsk–Ladyzhynka–Uman. The Hungarian troops clashed with the troops of the 209th Mountain Rifle Regiment, belonged to Colonel Shepetov's 96th Mountain Rifle Division. The Hungarian troops became the southern cornerstone of the encirclement, and were in position to close the 40km-wide gap in the encirclement around Uman. On the morning of 1 August, the commands of the Soviet 6th and 12th armies (from 28 July, the remnants of the 6th and 12th armies and the 2nd Mechanized Corps were combined as the Ponedelin Group) sent a joint communication to the command of the Southern Front, with a copy sent to Stalin (Glantz 2011: 121). In it they stated that the situation was critical, as they were completely encircled and disintegration threatened; they lacked reserves and ammunition, and their fuel supplies were running out.

ABOVE LEFT
Mounted and motorized
elements of the 4th Hussar
Regiment pass under a
welcome arch erected
by members of the local
population in July 1941.
As the Hungarian troops
advanced deeper into Ukraine,
towards the River Bug, they
found that conditions had
deteriorated and the attitude
of the local population
towards them had become
more hostile. No built roads
existed. The collectivization
of the small villages meant
that churches were used for
storage or as animal shelters,
which deeply shocked the
Hungarians and confirmed
their prejudices about the
Bolshevik system. The NKVD-
organized partisan movement
was also a real threat. (Péter
Illésfalvi)

ABOVE RIGHT
Hungarian riflemen cross a
creek on a makeshift bridge
built from carts. A number
of the soldiers carry metal
ammunition boxes for the
squad light machine gun.
(Author's collection)

Despite this, Tyulenev assured Stalin that the situation would be restored by an attack towards the Ponedelin Group made by the fresh 223rd Rifle Division from the north-east and elements of the 18th Army from the south, while denying any supply difficulties. Among the encircled Soviet units was the 1st Communist Regiment, composed of freshly joined Komsomol members mobilized from Dnepropetrovsk. In the event it was not possible to come to the help of Ponedelin's beleaguered forces, which were falling apart. On 1 August, units of the 18th Army continued to conduct defensive battles on their own, on a front Kolodistoye–Moshchena–Savran, holding the region of Getmanovka with a single rifle regiment. Under flanking blows of German and Hungarian units, the divisions of the 17th Rifle Corps were forced to retreat to the line Krasnogorka–Moldovka, south-west of Golovanevsk.

The temporary withdrawal of German mountain troops from Golovanevsk was regarded by the Soviet command as a retreat. At about 1900hrs on 1 August, units of the 17th Rifle Corps broke into the south-eastern and north-eastern quarters of the town. This Soviet penetration was not supported effectively by the remaining corps units, and their attacks were halted by the fierce resistance of elements of 4. Gebirgs-Division. This allowed the Germans to undertake a counter-attack with elements of 52. AK and the Mobile Corps during the evening of 1 August. Unable to stand the pressure of German forces, by the end of 1 August units of the 18th Army had been forced back to the line Krasnogorka–Moldovka. At around 2100hrs the Soviet forces received an order to retreat to Pervomaysk.

The 1st Motorized Rifle Brigade formed the spearhead of the advancing Mobile Corps on 1 August, crossing the River Bug at Gayvoron closely followed by the 2nd Motorized Rifle Brigade and the 1st Cavalry Brigade. At 0900hrs on 2 August the 1st Reconnaissance and 1st Motorized Rifle battalions attacked the heights west of Moldovka. When the Soviet forces counter-attacked from the village with 12 light tanks the Hungarian 37mm 36M anti-tank guns and the 20mm turret-mounted anti-tank rifles of the 39M Csaba armoured cars knocked out four Soviet tanks and the rest aborted the attack. With the support of the 1st Reconnaissance Battalion the Hungarian motorized rifles captured Moldovka in a rapid attack lasting less than half an hour.

On 2 August Colonel Ferenc Bissza assumed command of the 2nd Motorized Rifle Brigade, taking over from Major-General Vörös. Also on 2 August, 4. Gebirgs-Division split the compressed Soviet forces into two parts near Uman, and 125. Infanterie-Division seized the Uman–Novo Archangel'sk road. In the region of Novo Archangel'sk–Oksanino–Dubova–Ternovka German aerial reconnaissance identified the assembly of 1,400 Soviet trucks and horsed vehicles preparing for a breakthrough. German troops of 16. Panzer-Division entered Pervomaysk and linked up with the troops of AOK 17. As a result, two rings of encirclement had formed around the Ponedelin Group.

From the north and east of Novo Archangel'sk, units of 16., 11. and 9. Panzer-Divisionen advanced, as well as 16. Infanterie-Division (mot.) and SS-Division (mot.) *Leibstandarte-SS Adolf Hitler*. From the west, 297., 24., 125. and 97. Infanterie-Divisionen approached. To the south, 1. and 4. Gebirgs-Divisionen, 257. and 96. Infanterie-Divisionen, 100. and 101. leichte Infanterie-Divisionen, units of the Mobile Corps, the Romanian Cavalry Corps and the Italian 9th Infantry Division *Pasubio* were operating. In all, 22 Axis divisions were operating against the Ponedelin Group, in the vicinity of Pervomaysk, Uman and Kirovograd. The Luftwaffe's IV. Fliegerkorps mounted ongoing aerial attacks against Red Army units trying to escape from the trap.

On 5 August the 1st Motorized Rifle Brigade was ensconced in Pervomaysk, with several battalions holding the crossings over the River Bug, south of the town. The Hungarians faced potential attack from three directions: to the north, where trapped Soviet units at Uman frantically tried to break out southwards; to the south, where Soviet troops were attempting to withdraw north-eastwards, while the 1st Motorized Rifle Brigade and the 1st Cavalry Brigade occupied the only crossings available to the enemy; and to the east, where Soviet forces were trying to send reinforcements to relieve their trapped troops. The 1st Cavalry Brigade occupied the river crossings for a distance of some 50km along the northern bank of the Bug. To the north of Pervomaysk, 101. leichte Infanterie-Division and 257. Infanterie-Division provided flanking cover.

These Soviet infantrymen armed with submachine guns may belong to an assault detachment; such units enjoyed a firepower advantage over the Hungarian motorized rifles. (russiainphoto.ru/A Ryumin/ MAMM/MDF)

1 0945hrs: Having been ordered by Major-General Antal Vattay, the commander of the 1st Cavalry Brigade, to reconnoitre the Soviet break-out attempt, Ensign László Merész and his two Hungarian 39M Csaba armoured cars bypass the resting staff and the supply columns of 257. Infanterie-Division.

2 1000hrs: South of Golovanevsk, Hungarian armoured cars bump into three Red Army cavalry squadrons; two of the squadrons are annihilated.

3 1045hrs: Merész deploys his two armoured cars towards the forested area, placing them along the road in an ambush position.

4 1100hrs: The Hungarian armoured cars open fire on 20 Soviet trucks driving south. A Red Army rifle company attacks out of the forest. Two Soviet tanks clash with the armoured cars.

5 1130hrs: Merész radios back that he is running out of ammunition and retreats in order to replenish his stocks of ammunition.

6 Morning: The observation post of the commander of the 6th Army, Lieutenant-General Muzychenko, is situated just 600m from Merész's armoured cars.

7 1200hrs: A third armoured car and a bicycle platoon arrive and stabilize the Hungarian positions alongside the railway line. The Hungarians destroy the infiltrated Soviet troops.

Battlefield environment

Amid hilly terrain the valleys were marshy and forest, primarily with deciduous trees; low areas were bogs while the higher ground was covered with pine trees. It was ideal terrain for hiding, evading or mounting ambushes. The weather had improved somewhat, with less rainfall, meaning that the muddy roads dried up.

Hungarian artillery cross the River Bug in July 1941. The bridge panels of the 33M military bridge system rest on pontoons. This 37M Hansa-Lloyd artillery tractor is towing a 37M light howitzer. (NL-HaNA)

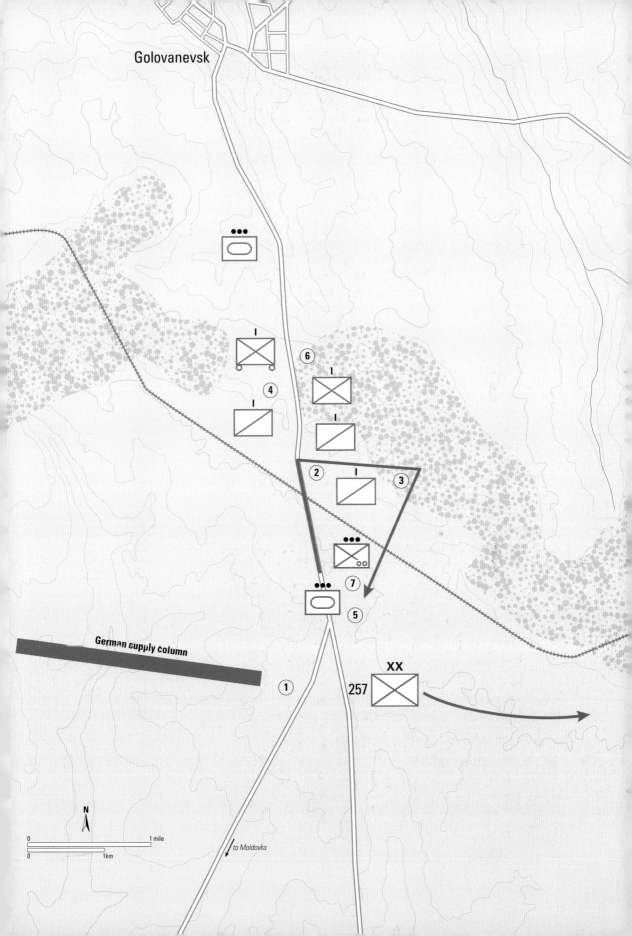

Golovanevsk

German supply column

1

257

XX

2

3

4

5

6

7

N

0   1 mile

0   1km

to Moldovka

INTO COMBAT

The Soviet 6th Army planned to break out of the encirclement by collecting several of its remaining tanks in a special task force. The units of 1. and 4. Gebirgs-Divisionen failed to stop Soviet forces from breaking through during the night of 5/6 August, when a contingent led by Muzychenko and composed of about 4,000 soldiers of the 141st and 190th Rifle divisions supported by ten tanks of the 44th Tank Division broke through the positions of 4. Gebirgs-Division at Kopenkovata and headed towards Golovanevsk. After a march of 20km the Soviet troops reached the village, but instead of the 18th Army, they encountered German troops of LII. Armeekorps and the Hungarian Mobile Corps. Demoralized by the constant retreat, the air strikes of the Luftwaffe and the swift advance of the Axis forces, the 96th Mountain Rifle and the 169th Rifle divisions disintegrated and ceased to exist as cohesive units.

The 1st and 2nd Motorized Rifle and 1st Cavalry brigades were grouped exactly on the path of the attacking Soviet troops, with the 1st Cavalry Brigade positioned closest to the Red Army units. On the sunny morning of 6 August one of the Hungarian static signals posts, responsible for transmitting messages from the brigades to corps headquarters, reported that the Soviet forces had broken out of the encirclement north of Uman; heavy small-arms fire could be heard. According to further reports, the Soviet forces were moving around the forests of Golovanevsk alongside the railway line towards the rear echelon of the 1st Cavalry Brigade.

Wishing to gain a clearer understanding of the situation, Major-General Antal Vattay, the commander of the 1st Cavalry Brigade, decided to send a

This destroyed Soviet ZiS-5 truck and its deceased crew were photographed at Golovanevsk after Ensign Merész's patrol on 6 August 1941. (Fortepan/Fedő Károly Hajdú)

patrol to locate the enemy. Vattay summoned the patrol commander, Ensign László Merész, a young reserve officer of the Armoured Car Company of the 1st Armoured Cavalry Battalion, to his headquarters at 0830hrs. Vattay personally briefed Merész to reconnoitre the area around Golovanevsk and sweep out the hiding Red Army units located there.

Merész had under his command his armoured-car platoon – three 39M Csaba armoured cars – reinforced with a bicycle platoon. The plan was to meet the bicycle platoon at a given road junction at Moldovka and proceed together towards the possible Soviet infiltration positions. In the event, the bicycle platoon did not arrive on time, and so Merész left one of his armoured cars behind to wait for the 'rubber hussars' (the nickname of the Hungarian bicycle troops) and continued with his task. During his movement the patrol passed the resting staff and the supply columns of 257. Infanterie-Division. The Germans were parked alongside the road without any close protection. Merész saluted the German divisional commander, Generalmajor Carl Sachs, who was sitting in his command car.

The two Hungarian armoured cars accelerated and drove quickly in the countryside, crossing a railway intersection. Suddenly, south of Golovanevsk, they bumped into unidentified cavalry troops. Initially believing them to be Romanian, Merész halted and from the turret of his armoured car addressed the officer in charge of the cavalry in German. Then his second armoured car arrived; luckily, its driver spoke Slovakian and was able to identify that the cavalry answered in Russian – they belonged to the Red Army. Merész immediately ordered his platoon to open fire with their 20mm anti-tank rifles and 8mm machine guns on the advancing Soviet cavalry. The cavalrymen panicked and dead horses and soldiers littered the roadside; within a few minutes two Soviet cavalry squadrons were beaten back with severe casualties.

Merész managed to capture two Soviet cavalrymen and brought them back to the German troops for interrogation. When questioned, the prisoners confirmed that their role was to find gaps in the encirclement through which to mount a breakthrough attempt. The two advancing Red Army cavalry squadrons were followed by a third one. Based on the information

Four 39M Csaba armoured cars of the Armoured Car Company, 1st Armoured Cavalry Battalion, commanded by Ensign László Merész, are pictured at Golovanevsk on 6 August 1941. (Péter Illésfalvi)

Ambush at Golovanevsk

On 5 August, roughly 4,000 Soviet soldiers broke through the Axis lines and headed towards the Hungarian 1st Cavalry Brigade. A Hungarian reconnaissance patrol led by Ensign László Merész of the 1st Armoured Cavalry Battalion was ordered on 6 August to locate the enemy. At about 1000hrs, three Red Army cavalry squadrons bumped into the Hungarian 39M Csaba armoured cars, with deadly consequences for the horsemen and their mounts. Roughly an hour later, a Soviet motor column heading south was ambushed by the Hungarian armoured cars, which opened fire at close range. The first Soviet truck was halted by direct hits; the following vehicles ran into the first one. South of the road, about two companies of Soviet infantry advance from the woods. Armed with Mosin-Nagant rifles with fixed bayonets, the riflemen wear SSh-39 helmets and the usual Soviet kit, with knee-length boots. An NCO is trying to rally his men; he is armed with an SVT-38 semi-automatic rifle and wears the appropriate magazine pouches.

received, 257. Infanterie-Division was alerted and prepared for the incoming Soviet attack.

When Merész reported his contact with the enemy to his brigade commander at 1030hrs, Vattay alerted his brigade. Merész did not wait for new orders; he deployed his two armoured cars in the forested area alongside the road in an ambush position. Very soon they detected a Soviet column of 20 trucks driving south. The armoured cars opened fire at close range (30–40m). The leading Soviet truck was halted by direct hits; the following trucks ran into the first one. The Hungarian armoured cars drove along the road and constantly suppressed the enemy with anti-tank rifle and machine-gun fire. Suddenly, large number of Soviet infantry advanced from the woods south of the road; the Hungarians repelled them with fire and the confused infantry fell back to the forest.

Reserve 2nd Lieutenant László Merész was decorated and promoted for his leadership and bravery at the battle of Golovanevsk in 1941. (Péter Illésfalvi)

Without warning, two Soviet tanks appeared on the battlefield. Although Merész's lightly armoured vehicles were no match for the Soviet vehicles (probably BT or T-26 light tanks), the Hungarian armoured cars did not retreat. The armoured cars immediately engaged the Soviet tanks, hitting the first one with their 20mm anti-tank rifles. Merész's vehicle was also hit; his driver, Lance Corporal Ferenc Toldi, was seriously wounded and the armoured car slipped into a ditch. The wounded driver was replaced and Merész's armoured car retreated to evacuate his wounded driver. Meanwhile Candidate-Sergeant László Cserniczky's armoured car covered the evacuation with continuous fire. The Soviet tanks did not follow the Hungarian armoured cars, but instead simply disengaged. The seriously injured Hungarian driver was air-evacuated by the Germans and directly flown to

László Merész

László Merész was born on 17 January 1915, in Kaposvár. In 1938 he graduated at the University of Economics of Budapest and worked at the Hungarian National Bank. Completing his compulsory military service with the armoured reconnaissance troops, as a university graduate he attended the reserve officer-cadet training course. He was called up and took part in the peaceful operation in Transylvania and the Yugoslavian Campaign. Merész joined the 1st Armoured Cavalry Battalion (1st Cavalry Brigade) at Nyíregyháza in spring 1941; he was appointed a platoon commander in the battalion's Armoured Car Company holding the rank of reserve ensign.

In the early days of August 1941, German and Hungarian forces crossed the River Bug and reached the Stalin Line. On 6 August Merész was ordered to carry out a reconnaissance towards to the Soviet troops trapped near Uman. When his armoured cars encountered two Red Army cavalry squadrons south of Golovanevsk, Merész, acting on his own initiative, repelled and destroyed the enemy forces. On 28 January 1944 – more than two years after the action – he was decorated with the Officer's Golden Medal for Bravery.

Merész was promoted to 2nd lieutenant and demobilized in December 1941. In 1944, he was recalled and served as a company commander in the 3rd Tank Regiment. He ended the war with his unit in Austria and was captured by the US Army. After the war he did not return to Hungary, which was under Soviet occupation; he feared reprisals based on his military record. Instead, he moved to London and in 1951 emigrated to Australia, where he died on 13 November 1997.

Warsaw, where he was operated on; he lost one eye but survived and was decorated for his part in the action.

By 1130hrs, Merész reported back that he had run out of ammunition and planned to retreat to replenish his ammunition stocks. The third armoured car and the bicycle platoon arrived at about midday, stabilized and sealed the gap and destroyed the infiltrated Soviet troops. During the action the Hungarian armoured cars fired 12,000 machine-gun cartridges and 720 20mm anti-tank shells. For his leadership and bravery, Merész was decorated with the highest Hungarian military decoration for valour, the Officer's Golden Medal for Bravery, and also received the Iron Cross from the Germans.

According to the two interrogated Soviet prisoners, this attempted breakthrough was led by the commander of the 6th Army, Lieutenant-

Ivan N. Muzychenko

Ivan Nikolaevich Muzychenko was born on 20 October 1901 in Rostov-on-Don. Having joined the Russian Army in 1917, he fought in the Red Army during the Russian Civil War (1917–22); he was decorated with the Order of the Red Star and was wounded five times. In 1927 he graduated from the Cavalry Commanders' Advanced Training Course. He commanded the 21st Cossack Regiment and the 4th Cossack Division before becoming a training instructor in 1938. He emerged from the military purges unscathed.

Appointed commander of the 4th Rifle Division, he fought in the Winter War (1939–40). In July 1940, aged 39 and after just three months in command of the 6th Rifle Corps, he was given command of the 6th Army.

During the battle of Uman, the 6th and 12th armies were encircled. On 6 August, Muzychenko observed from his tactical command post his troops trying to break through. When the arriving Hungarian armoured cars repelled the Soviet forces and sealed the gap, Muzychenko's observation post was just 600m from the Hungarian ensign commanding two armoured cars.

According to Soviet sources (Maslov 2001: 50), Muzychenko was wounded, possibly on 6 August, and captured by the Germans. He was liberated by US Army troops on 29 April 1945 and returned to Moscow. After months of screening he was cleared in December 1945 and returned to the Red Army., retiring in 1947. He died in Moscow on 8 December 1970.

ABOVE LEFT
A Soviet machine-gun team pull their M1910/30 Maxim medium machine gun on its two-wheeled Sokolov mounting amid terrain similar to that encountered at Moldovka on 6 August 1941. The M1910 had a distinctive water jacket and a Sokolov mounting; the gun and the carriage weighed 74kg. (russiainphoto.ru/Sergey Korshunov)

ABOVE RIGHT
These Soviet machine-gunners armed with an M1910/30 Maxim medium machine gun and rifles wear sidecaps, ankle boots, puttees and rolled greatcoats according to regulations. (russiainphoto.ru/MAMM/MDF)

General Muzychenko, who was later taken prisoner; his observation post was just 600m from Merész's armoured cars.

The Germans initially lacked combat troops to counter the break-out attempts mounted by the Soviet forces. During the afternoon, German reinforcements began to arrive near Golovanevsk. According to the Soviet sources, at 1500hrs Artillerie-Regiment 83 (4. Gebirgs-Division) dug in on the northern outskirts, a construction company deployed 1.5km to the west, and a company from the headquarters troops of 52. AK covered the road from the railway station to the town (Nuzhdin 2015: 248). A Hungarian tank company took up position at a road intersection south-east of Golovanevsk, and at 1700hrs one heavy field howitzer from 11./AR 83 was transferred there.

On 7 August, moving east, the remnants of the 190th Rifle Division engaged several times in minor skirmishes with the Axis forces, the most significant of which occurred during the Soviet effort to cross the Golovanevsk–Pervomaysk road. Small groups from other divisions joined the party from the 190th Rifle Division en route. On the night of 7/8 August, they crossed the River Sinyukha near the village of Plosko-Zabugskoye, and later successfully crossed the Soviet front line into the defensive zone of the 18th Army.

The encircled Soviet forces were forced to surrender at Uman on 8 August; the Germans captured 103,000 prisoners of war from 25 divisions and captured or destroyed 317 tanks, 858 artillery pieces and 242 anti-tank and anti-aircraft guns. Major-General Proshkin's 58th Mountain Rifle Division was effectively annihilated. During the fighting, two Soviet army commanders, four corps commanders and 11 divisional commanders were captured, including Major-General Ponedelin, commander of the 12th Army, and Major-General Kirillov, commander of the 13th Rifle Corps of the 12th Army, both captured on 7 August. Ponedelin was personally interrogated by Generaloberst Ewald von Kleist, the commander of Panzergruppe 1. Major-General Nikolai N. Belov, the commander of the 15th Rifle Division (former 15th Tank Division), had been wounded on 4 August but refused to be evacuated by air; he was killed in action by a shell fragment on 9 August near the village of Podvysokoe.

Khortytsia

1–6 September 1941

BACKGROUND TO BATTLE

After concluding operations at Uman, the Axis forces continued to pursue their objectives. The Germans grouped 16. Panzer-Division and 16. Infanterie-Division (mot.) with the Mobile Corps as Battle Group Kempf, tasked with the capture of Nikolayev. The Germans wanted to prevent the retreating Soviet forces of the 9th Army and the Independent Coastal Army from merging.

At 1600hrs on 18 August, demolition specialists of the 157th NKVD Regiment used 20 tonnes of explosive to blow a 120m-wide hole in the Dnepr Hydroelectric Dam. A wave several dozen metres high swept away everything situated in the floodplain of the Dnepr – locals, refugees and soldiers alike (Bergström 2016: 154). The Soviet forces' main goal was to delay the Axis offensive and cover the evacuation of the factories, especially in the lower Dnepr and Donbas region in Ukraine. The stubborn defence of the Southwestern Front paid dividends: German efforts to strengthen their troops advancing towards Moscow were hampered and time was bought for the Soviets to dismantle their factory machinery and evacuate it to Siberia, out of reach of the Germans.

Following their long advance, the Hungarian mobile troops were allowed a brief period of rest from 19 August. The Mobile Corps had to achieve operational readiness by 27 August to deploy from Krivoy Rog to the River Dnepr. Panzergruppe 1 established a bridgehead at Dnepropetrovsk on the Dnepr on 26 August. South of this point two German divisions screened the riverbank; called in to replace them, the Mobile Corps would be assigned the mission of guarding the southern flank of Heeresgruppe Süd.

On the Soviet side, elements of the Southern Front confronted the Hungarian troops. The 12th Army, now commanded by Major-General

Part of the thin Hungarian defence line at the Dnepr, this camouflaged sentry post is manned by four soldiers wearing 35M steel helmets and armed with 35M rifles and a 31M light machine gun. Along the Hungarian front line the field posts were located 800–3,000m apart from each other. During the hours of daylight, the areas between the field posts were monitored by visual observation and patrolling. At night-time the Hungarian troops tried to monitor the lines by listening and patrolling. The gaps between the Hungarian positions were sporadically blocked by anti-personnel mines. (Fortepan/ Kókány Jenő)

Ivan V. Galanin (the former commander of the 17th Rifle Corps), had the 270th and 274th Rifle divisions, the 11th Tank Division and the 268th and 374th Corps Artillery regiments. The deteriorating quality of the rifle elements of the 12th Army reflected the growing Red Army losses. As the Soviet authorities strove to replace casualties, half-trained and inadequately armed units were thrown into the battle. The 270th Rifle Division, including the 973rd, 975th and 977th Rifle regiments and the 810th Artillery Regiment, began forming on 10 July under the command of Colonel Zaki Kutlin; composed of militiamen and reservists, the division assembled east of the Dnepr bend in about a month. The 274th Rifle Division, fielding the 961st, 963rd and 965th Rifle regiments and the 814th Artillery Regiment, began forming on 10 July at Zaporozh'ye. The 274th Rifle Division was untrained and incomplete when it reached the front line, having never received its full complement of artillery or anti-tank weapons; it suffered heavy losses.

The city of Zaporozh'ye was an important industrial hub in the Soviet Union with steel and aluminium plants and a hydroelectric dam. The Soviet troops were determined to defend the city until its industrial machinery could be dismantled and transported to relative safety further east. According to Hungarian intelligence sources, the city itself was occupied by the 545th Security Division.

These Soviet forces faced the Hungarian 2nd Motorized Rifle Brigade and the Ankay-Anesini Group (Colonel Győző Ankay-Anesini), composed of the bicycle and motorized elements of the 1st Cavalry Brigade. The 18th Army, commanded by Lieutenant-General Andrei K. Smirnov, had the

17th and 55th Rifle corps, fielding the 96th Mountain Rifle Division, the 130th, 164th and 169th Rifle divisions and the 30th Cavalry Division plus the 437th Corps Artillery and 82nd Anti-Aircraft Artillery regiments. Of these, the 96th Mountain Rifle Division, the 30th Cavalry Division and the 437th Corps Artillery Regiment opposed the 1st Motorized Rifle Brigade at Nikopol. The Soviet forces were determined to keep their position until the factory machinery was dismantled and removed.

From 30 August, the Mobile Corps was assigned to defend the River Dnepr south of Dnepropetrovsk. The Hungarians were given a front 200km long, but they were too weak to set up a rigid defence. The commander of the Mobile Corps organized a token defence along the river to monitor Soviet activity. The dismounted bicycle, cavalry and motorized rifle troops occupied strongholds along the river and the motorized and armoured elements acted as mobile reserves.

Assigned a 55km-long defence line including the island of Khortytsia, the 2nd Motorized Rifle Brigade had six battalions and 14 artillery batteries. The artillery grouped behind the 2nd Motorized Rifle Brigade was reinforced with a motorized light-artillery battalion and the corps-level medium-artillery batteries. The Ankay-Anesini Group (composed of the 13th and 14th Bicycle battalions, the 1st Armoured Cavalry Battalion, two Bofors-equipped anti-aircraft batteries, two anti-tank companies and the 3rd Motorized Artillery Battalion) was assigned a 45km-long defence line north of the island of Khortytsia. The 1st Motorized Rifle Brigade (three battalions and four batteries) was located to the south of the 2nd Motorized Rifle Brigade, covering a 100km-long stretch of the riverbank. Two (mounted) cavalry battalions were kept in reserve at Tomakovka, but the rest of the cavalry troops were dismounted and dispersed among the rifle units along the riverbank. The Mobile Corps' tactical headquarters was also located at Tomakovka.

The most critical point of the defence was the island of Khortytsia: 12km long and 1.5–2km wide, it was crossed by a railway line connected with bridges to both riverbanks of the Dnepr. The 5th Motorized Rifle Battalion and the 12th Bicycle Battalion replaced the German units on the island on 29–30 July. The 8km-long defence line of the 5th Motorized Rifle Battalion was manned by 2½ rifle companies, with one half-company kept in reserve. These Hungarian troops were supported by two batteries of light howitzers and one of medium howitzers. The southern part of the island could not be occupied due to the presence of German minefields planted on the beach before the reduction of the water level. The Soviet troops held a significant advantage in that the eastern bank of the river was higher and so provided them with a commanding view of the Hungarian positions. The Soviet forces deployed train-mounted artillery batteries to bombard the Hungarian positions.

The Hungarian defences were weak and sporadic everywhere. For example, the 2nd Company of the 13th Bicycle Battalion (Ankay-Anesini Group) was required to defend a 12km-long sector with four platoons armed with just 11 light machine guns and one anti-tank rifle. The Hungarians dug in the island were supported by two light- and one medium-artillery batteries. Facing them were the 270th and 274th Rifle divisions, the 11th Tank Division and the 268th and 374th Corps Artillery regiments of the 12th Army.

MAP KEY

1 **2200hrs, 1 September:** Soviet troops infiltrate the south-eastern part of the island of Khortytsia and clash with the Hungarian 2nd Company, 5th Motorized Rifle Battalion.

2 **0545hrs, 2 September:** A company of the 965th Rifle Regiment (274th Rifle Division) attacks the position of the IV Platoon of the 1st Company, 5th Motorized Rifle Battalion.

3 **2 September:** The 2nd Company, 5th Motorized Rifle Battalion reports that about four Red Army battalions have crossed the River Dnepr and dug in the south-eastern part of the island.

4 **Afternoon, 3 September:** Hungarian attacks to restore the situation collapse and on 4 September the pressure of the Soviet forces steadily grows.

5 **0030hrs, 5 September:** Soviet troops mount a strong attack on the defensive positions of the 3rd Company,

5th Motorized Rifle Battalion and the 12th Bicycle Battalion on the island.

6 **1700hrs, 5 September:** The Soviet attackers break the defence line of the 1st Company, 5th Motorized Rifle Battalion.

7 **2300hrs, 5 September:** Major-General Miklós leaves Colonel Benda's tactical headquarters on the island, having categorically forbidden the evacuation of the Hungarian position.

8 **Evening, 6 September:** After Colonel Benda finally orders the withdrawal of the Hungarian troops from Khortytsia, the defenders move via the bridge and ferries to the western side of the Dnepr.

9 **6 September:** The 14th Bicycle Battalion makes a final dash on the central road bridge to occupy a bridgehead on the island around the bridge. The battalion's sappers prepare the bridge over the Dnepr for demolition.

Battlefield environment

The Dnepr had a wide floodplain with heavy vegetation, meaning that it was difficult to monitor and control. Owing to the demolition of the dam at Zaporozh'ye, the water level of the Dnepr had fallen by 10m. In some places the river could be crossed on foot. The substantial vegetation in the floodplain, and on the islands and sandbanks provided ideal hiding places and infiltration points for the Soviet troops. The weather was initially hot and dry; it was difficult to get drinking water. By the end of September, however, the weather became rainy and cold.

The area along the river was packed with wandering Soviet soldiers trying to reach friendly lines. The Hungarians found

that it was difficult to determine who was a civilian and who was a combatant. During the hours of darkness, Soviet patrols crossed the river and tested the Hungarian sentries. The Soviet soldiers escaping from the encirclement and male civilians also crossed the river in an effort to reach their own troops. As a countermeasure the Hungarians attempted to prohibit the locals from going to the river, but this proved to be impracticable. Eventually, the local population was checked and screened; hidden Soviet soldiers, deserters and would-be partisans were arrested and taken into custody.

Hungarian troops man a blocking position. The 37mm 36M anti-tank gun team is covered by a 31M light machine gun. The metal boxes each contained five spare magazines for the light machine gun. (HM HIM 78364)

INTO COMBAT

By 1 September, the Hungarian troops had taken over the entire sector from the Germans. Personnel of the brigade headquarters of the 2nd Motorized Rifle Brigade had a strange encounter with a group of male Soviet civilians in the town of Shirokoye on 1 September. According to a Hungarian combat report, the men pretended to surrender, then attacked the Hungarians, only to be neutralized by the close-protection platoon.

During the evening of 1 September Soviet troops infiltrated the south-eastern part of the island of Khortytsia and at 2200hrs clashed with the 2nd Company, 5th Motorized Rifle Battalion. The ensuing skirmishes lasted until midnight. Hostilities continued on the island on 2 September. The 1st Company, 5th Motorized Rifle Battalion, reported via field telephone that at 0545hrs a Soviet company attacked the position of its IV Platoon. Soviet artillery laid a heavy barrage on the boundary between the positions of the 1st and 2nd companies. The battalion commander, Lieutenant-Colonel Lőrinc Latorczay, deployed his reserve half-company to stabilize the situation. The Soviet forces fielded about 700 troops to evict the Hungarians from their positions. The Hungarian motorized rifles repelled the attack, killing 12 Soviet soldiers and capturing 11: they were reservists aged between 40 and 45 years old, belonging to the 965th Rifle Regiment (274th Rifle Division). According to Hungarian interrogation reports, the captured Soviet soldiers stated that they had departed from Kharkov on 20 August. The Soviet commanders' aim was to capture the island in order to use it as a jumping-off position for further attacks.

The battalion commander sent out patrols to get a clear view on the situation. In the meantime, the 2nd Company, 5th Motorized Rifle Battalion, reported that about two Soviet battalions had crossed the river and dug in the island. Lieutenant-Colonel Latorczay, the battalion commander, requested artillery strikes on the south-eastern part of the island. Colonel Benda organized a company-strong force from elements of the 4th and 5th Motorized Rifle battalions to restore the situation. The Hungarian counter-attack started on the afternoon of 3 September but collapsed in the face of heavy fire from the Soviet infantry and artillery.

On 3 September the defensive sector of the 1st Motorized Rifle Brigade was subjected to Soviet air raids and artillery barrages from the 437th Corps Artillery Regiment. When the Soviet artillery preparation ended at 1500hrs, troops of Colonel Shepetov's 96th Mountain Rifle Division tried to cross the river in small wooden boats. The Hungarian units responded with concentrated small-arms and artillery fire: 7–8 Soviet barges were capsized and the rest turned back. Meanwhile, at Dovgolovka a Hungarian platoon position of the 2nd Motorized Rifle Battalion was attacked from behind by Soviet partisans, most probably soldiers escaping from the encirclement. The besieged platoon was relieved by the battalion reserve. According to Hungarian combat reports, the Soviet forces engaged lost 50 killed and 30 captured soldiers.

During 4 September the pressure exerted by the Soviet forces grew steadily: the Hungarian heavy weapons began to break down due to sustained use and several junior officers reported that their men were totally exhausted by the nonstop Soviet activity. The Red Army troops mounted bayonet charges

On the western bank of the Dnepr, members of a Hungarian machine-gun team man an 07/31M Schwarzlose medium machine gun with its distinctive flash suppressor. The 07/31M's rate of fire was 400rd/min and the weapon was fed by 250-round ammunition belts. It is late September; these troops wear gloves and greatcoats due to the cool weather. (Author's collection)

under cover of darkness, seemingly oblivious to their own casualties, causing severe demoralization among the Hungarian defenders.

At 0030hrs on 5 September, under heavy artillery preparation and masked by a smokescreen, a strong force of Soviet troops attacked the positions of the 3rd Company of the 5th Motorized Rifle Battalion and the 12th Bicycle Battalion on the island. The Soviet troops pushed back the Hungarians some 400m. The Hungarians deployed their reserves – the 4th Motorized Rifle Battalion sent in one-and-a-half rifle companies – but the original position could not be restored. The soldiers of the 5th Motorized Rifle Battalion were totally exhausted by six days of constant Soviet activity. From 0600hrs the Soviet troops continued the attack against the troops of the 5th Motorized Rifle Battalion. The Soviet pressure continued; at 1700hrs the defence line of the 1st Company was broken by the enemy. As combat intensified on the island, Colonel Bissza mobilized all of his brigade's reserves – the 6th Motorized Rifle Battalion and the 14th Bicycle Battalion – to relieve the Hungarian troops on the island. It was the crisis point of the battle, but the Hungarian troops were too exhausted. The commander of the 14th Bicycle Battalion, Colonel Zoltán Bartha, had a nervous breakdown and his second-in-command reported sick before the attack. The commander of the 6th Motorized Rifle Battalion, Lieutenant-Colonel Keményfy, refused to lead his troops in a pointless suicide counter-attack.

The commander of the Mobile Corps requested permission from Panzergruppe 1 to withdraw from the island of Khortytsia. The Germans refused it and promised German troops to replace the Hungarian 1st Motorized Rifle Brigade, which in return could strengthen the defence on the island. The German force relocation was too late, however. Major-General Miklós visited Colonel Benda at his tactical headquarters on the island and stayed there until 2300hrs on 5 September: he categorically forbade the evacuation of the Hungarian position.

The Hungarian situation on the island deteriorated further on 6 September. The battle group commander, Colonel Benda, also had a nervous breakdown and at about 1900hrs ordered the withdrawal of the Hungarian troops from Khortytsia to the western side of the Dnepr via the bridge and ferries. The 14th Bicycle Battalion made a final dash on the central road bridge to occupy a bridgehead on the island, and the battalion sappers prepared the bridge over the Dnepr for demolition.

During the 1–6 September fighting, the 5th Motorized Rifle Battalion suffered heavy casualties: two officers and 23 men were killed, nine officers and 166 men were wounded and 52 men were reported missing in action.

Upset that the Hungarian evacuation had occurred in spite of his orders, Generaloberst Kleist requested an investigation and pressed for punishment of the Hungarian commander in charge. Generalleutnant Heinrich Clössner, commander of 25. Infanterie-Division (mot.), was sent ahead to investigate the circumstances; Major-General Miklós was also ordered to clarify the situation. The investigation concluded that the evacuation from Khortytsia was prompted by the activities of overwhelming Soviet forces and the exhaustion of the Hungarian defenders.

On 6 September, the 1st Motorized Rifle Battalion attacked the units of the 96th Mountain Rifle Division and the 127th and 138th Cavalry regiments of the 30th Cavalry Division lodged south of Novokyivka. These Soviet units were supported by gunboats of the Dnepr River Flotilla. The depleted Hungarian motorized rifles were reinforced with one tank platoon of the 9th Bicycle/Light Tank Battalion and the brigade's movement-control company. The Hungarian troops desperately charged the Soviet positions. One Hungarian anti-tank company advanced and fired at close range with their 37mm anti-tank guns at the Soviet troops. The Hungarian 38M Toldi light tanks flanked the enemy. Finally the men of the movement-control company and the motorized riflemen broke the resistance of the Soviet troops in hand-to-hand combat. By 1100hrs the riverbank was cleared of Soviet troops: according to Hungarian combat reports, the Soviet losses were five officers and 120 enlisted men killed and 120 soldiers were captured. The 1st Motorized Rifle Battalion lost ten killed, including one sergeant and two officer-candidate sergeants. At 1000hrs on 6 September, elements of 16. Infanterie-Division (mot.) started to replace the troops of the 1st Motorized Rifle Brigade.

The commander of the tankette platoon of the 13th Bicycle Battalion, 1st Lieutenant György Babics, counter-attacked the Soviet forces lodged in the Hungarian defences around Vovnigi on 7 September. The counter-attack was carried out by two sapper squads and supported by a captured Soviet machine gun, as the platoon's 35M FIAT Ansaldo tankettes were non-operable. Babics' force defeated the infiltrated Soviet forces.

In recognition of the reduced strength of the Hungarian defenders, the Soviet commanders decided to wear them down by mounting frequent small-scale river-crossing attempts, supported by air raids and the infiltration of diversionary groups. NKVD-organized partisan groups were also activated to keep the Hungarians under pressure.

The Hungarian river-defence positions were reorganized, with normal-sized defensive sectors being allocated to the motorized rifle brigades. Each brigade had one motorized rifle battalion, one movement-control company and 15 light tanks with one day's fuel in reserve. Each battalion in a defensive position was supported by one light-howitzer battery. A central artillery-support group and long-range artillery batteries were organized and concealed Bofors guns were emplaced to provide flanking fire.

From 7 September, the Hungarians also carried out missions behind the Soviet lines. Squad- and platoon-strength patrols infiltrated the island of Khortytsia, capturing prisoners and collecting information. At dawn on 20 September, a rifle squad of the 2nd Motorized Rifle Battalion crossed the Dnepr at the northern tip of the island. This patrol surprised a Soviet post and captured 12 soldiers before returning to the Hungarian positions at 0730hrs.

A Soviet officer armed with an RGD-33 fragmentation grenade and TT service pistol stalks a Hungarian observation post alongside the riverbank. (russiainphoto.ru/Victor Temin/MAMM/MDF)

On 17 September the Soviet troops tried to cross the river on boats at several points, but were repelled by the concentrated fire of the 1st and 2nd Motorized Rifle brigades. The Hungarians observed that those boats which tried to return to the Soviet-held side of the river were fired upon by NKVD blocking detachments. Forced to return to the attack, the Soviet boats were capsized or sunk.

On 19 September the staff officers of the Mobile Corps and the Italian 52nd Infantry Division *Torino* met to discuss the possibility of the takeover of the Hungarian positions by the Italians. In the event, this handing over of responsibilities did not occur.

The troops of the Southwestern Front were encircled by Panzergruppe 1 from the south and Panzergruppe 2 from the north, and on 19 September the Germans entered Kiev. The pressure on the Hungarian forces alongside the River Dnepr was correspondingly reduced. The island of Khortytsia was also evacuated by the Soviets and captured by Sicherungs-Regiment 4 on 6 October. The Soviet forces held the left bank of the river and the city for 45 days. During this time, workers were able to dismantle large amounts of heavy machinery, pack it up and load it onto railway wagons; some 9,600 wagons of equipment from Zaporozh'ye alone were successfully transported to Siberia.

The operation at Dnepr ended on 6 October. The Hungarians had lost nine officers and 148 men killed, 54 officers and 762 men wounded and 74 men missing in action. According to Hungarian reports based on prisoner interrogations, the Soviet forces engaged lost roughly 3,000 killed and 3,000 wounded officers and men during the period 30 August–6 October. The 270th Rifle Division alone lost 227 killed plus 828 wounded, missing or taken prisoner, as well as 2,460 men who were not present for other reasons, the majority of these probably absent without leave. The 6th Army initiated an investigation, but such significant losses must have stemmed in part from the division's broken fighting spirit.

To make good the Hungarian losses, the II and VII Bicycle battalions – both corps troops, hence the roman numerals in the unit titles – were deployed from Hungary and subordinated to the 2nd Motorized Rifle and

1st Cavalry brigades. By September each bicycle/light-tank battalion had only one company of 38M Toldi tanks. The 11th and 9th Bicycle/Light-Tank battalions were withdrawn and sent home, their 35–40 remaining light tanks and other vehicles being regrouped in one armoured field battalion based around the 1st Armoured Cavalry Battalion. From 27 September to 11 October, the Mobile Corps received a respite from the fighting in order to reorganize and recover, in an area south of Tomakovka. The depleted units of the motorized rifle brigades were reorganized: each was to be composed of three motorized rifle battalions, one reconnaissance battalion, signals and sapper companies, light-artillery batteries and allocated light tanks.

On 9 October, the Mobile Corps was subordinated to General der Infanterie Viktor von Schwendler's Battle Group, under AOK 17, to attack and occupy the Donets river basin. The weather turned against the attacking Axis forces, however: the autumn rainy season started on 7 October with pouring rain which turned the roads into impassable muddy tracks. Later, sleet and snow started to fall.

At a high military–political level the Hungarians petitioned the Germans to relieve the Mobile Corps so the Hungarian troops could be sent home. In fact, the Hungarians wanted to withdraw the Mobile Corps as early as the end of the Dnepr river-defence operation. The 1st Cavalry Brigade started its redeployment back to Hungary in early October. On 27 October, Miklós flew to Budapest to discuss the details of the withdrawal; Major-General Major was the acting corps commander.

The Hungarian forces reached the River Donets at Izyum on 28–29 October. On 2 November the reconnaissance patrols of the 1st Motorized Rifle Brigade entered Izyum and clashed with the Soviet rearguards. According to the German strategic planners, the Mobile Corps was tasked with taking Konstantinovka and later Voroshilovgrad; but at a political level the replacement of the Hungarian troops was approved by the Germans. As part of the deal, five Hungarian light brigades were deployed to Ukraine to perform occupational duties. These brigades were responsible for rear-area security but were understrength and lightly armed.

On 5 November, PzAOK 1 started its attack towards Rostov, defended by the 9th Army. Although the Germans opened a 30km-wide hole in the Soviet defences, their advance was slowed by the dogged resistance of Red Army units and on 11 November the Axis offensive halted. The newly formed 37th Army was sent by the Southern Front to reinforce the defence of Rostov. The sacrifice and heroism of the Red Army paid dividends: the new commander, Marshal Semen K. Timoshenko, strengthened the Soviet defences, prioritizing Rostov and pushing the Axis forces back to the River Mius. Within a week the momentum had swung in favour of the Red Army (Kirchubel 2003: 90).

This did not affect the troops of the Mobile Corps, however. From 6 November, 257. Infanterie-Division started to take over the position of the Mobile Corps. The Hungarians ceased operations and regrouped for redeployment to their home garrisons as soon as possible. Miklós and the Mobile Corps' chief-of-staff, Colonel Zoltán Zsedényi, visited Generaloberst Hermann Hoth, commander of AOK 17, on 16 November. Hoth hosted a farewell dinner for the Hungarian officers, praising the achievements of the Mobile Corps.

Analysis

LESSONS LEARNT: SOVIET

The Red Army suffered horrendous casualties during the first five months of the *Barbarossa* campaign, losing about 4 million soldiers with more than 1 million of these being killed in action and the rest taken prisoner, many of them subsequently dying in captivity. This represented 80 per cent of the total strength of the ground forces at the beginning of the war. In the period between 22 June and 16 November 1941 the Southwestern and Southern fronts lost 1,302,000 men. Nobody expected such high casualty figures (Krivosheev 1997: 112–19).

The Red Army identified the next problems related to its disastrous performance in the first six months of the Great Patriotic War (1941–45)

Soviet artillerymen eat their meal next to their 76.2mm M1936 (F-22) divisional guns. The gunners wear an SSh-39 helmet and *pilotka* sidecaps, M35 tunics and boots. (russiainphoto.ru/Victor Temin/MAMM/MDF)

as being incompetent leadership at every level, poorly trained command cadre and soldiers, inadequate use of the modern weaponry available and the hasty commitment to combat of poorly trained and equipped reserves (Glantz 2011: 209). Although these problems were identified, they could not be overcome quickly; the Red Army was still fighting for survival in 1941–42. It was quickly understood that battlefield communications had to improve drastically to provide the commanders with up-to-date information about friendly and enemy dispositions.

What the Soviet High Command could do was to implement stopgap measures to mitigate the imminent threats. The morale and discipline of Soviet troops were maintained with draconian measures such as military courts and the use of penal units; blocking detachments, tasked with preventing Soviet troops from evading combat, were organized at the front line and in the rear areas. Reductions in the number and strength of the subordinated units within each rifle division helped the inexperienced commanders to lead their units. Many divisions, heavily attrited by the 1941 fighting, were disbanded. The mountain-rifle divisions did not perform well due to their inadequate equipment and training. Upon the outbreak of war 19 mountain-rifle divisions existed, but by 1944 just four remained in service. The mechanized corps and their tank and motorized divisions were disbanded or already lost in the war. New independent mixed tank brigades were raised to fill the gaps.

Soviet infantry weapons, especially the automatic weapons, proved to be superior to their Hungarian equivalents. The 7.62mm PPD-40 and PPSh-41 submachine guns, although much fewer in number than later in the war, were prized war booty for the Hungarians. The SVT self-loading rifles were less reliable than the submachine guns, but were a useful part of Soviet fire teams alongside the DP light machine guns. Snipers armed with Mosin-Nagant rifles fitted with PU or PE telescopic sights proved to be lethally effective and could take out Hungarian officers, NCOs or other important targets such as radio operators and automatic-weapon crews. The Maxim medium machine gun was outdated, but offered similar performance to the Hungarian 07/31M Schwarzlose medium machine gun with superior mobility due to its two-wheeled carriage. The Soviet 45mm anti-tank guns could knock out any Hungarian armoured vehicle, as could the PTRD and PTRS anti-tank rifles. In terms of number and quality, the battalion-level 82mm mortars, regimental-level 120mm mortars and 76mm infantry guns provided superior fire support for Soviet rifle battalions operating in defence and counter-attacks. While the 45mm guns of the Soviet T-26 and BT light tanks and BA-6 armoured cars were superior to all Hungarian armoured vehicles, the Hungarian 37mm 36M anti-tank guns and 40mm 36M Bofors autocannon could knock them out. According to Hungarian reports, heavier Soviet armoured vehicles did not clash with the Hungarian troops; the Soviet T-28 and T-35 tanks were left behind due to technical breakdowns.

While in theory the automatic, heavy and support weapons of the Soviet rifle battalions/regiments were adequate, the crash-course training of the young or over-aged conscripts and volunteers and the shaky leadership exhibited by the Red Army's inexperienced and undertrained officers resulted in heavy casualties. Frequently faced with impossible combat situations, Soviet junior officers and battalion commanders had no choice other than to try to

live to fight another day, obeying strict orders that were frequently based on a complete misunderstanding of the actual situation. They had to lead their men while facing enormous pressure from above, threatened as they were by the prospect of questioning, investigation and possibly punishment for any decision that was not in line with the requirements of the higher echelons, irrespective of whether it was a sound military act.

Even so, the Soviet troops quickly adapted their defensive tactics based on delayed actions, ambushes and quick counter-attacks, followed by the rapid withdrawal of their forces from the battlefield. Frequently the Red Army units could choose the time and the place to set up ambushes, where they could concentrate superior numbers of troops and firepower. Sometimes it happened accidentally as a huge number of organized Soviet troops were moving between the front line and the rear of the Axis forces, trying to catch up with friendly forces. These units could appear out of the blue, outflanking and surprising the advancing Hungarians. The Red Army and the NKVD deployed covert forces to perform sabotage actions and target command posts and supply columns in the rear of the Hungarian combat formations.

While some Red Army units and individuals demonstrated a skilful and stubborn determination to fight the Hungarian troops, others were less dedicated and tried to avoid the confrontation, sometimes changing into civilian clothes and evading combat with the help of the local population. In general, though, the Hungarians had a high regard for the overall fighting skills of the Soviet troops, and the negative image of the Red Army's performance in the Winter War faded away quickly. It is important to note, though, that the unorthodox methods employed by Soviet soldiers were misinterpreted by the Hungarians as a wild, 'non-European' way of conducting war. As they became aware that Soviet forces were prepared to depart from the normal rules of engagement, employing measures such as disguising troops as civilians or

ABOVE LEFT
Soviet tankers reload the drum magazines of their 7.62mm Degtyaryov DT light machine gun. (russiainphoto.ru/Aron Zamsky/MAMM/MDF)

ABOVE RIGHT
A Soviet cavalry major briefs cavalry and tank officers before the break-out attempt at Uman, August 1941. The tank officers wear padded helmets and canvas overalls. (russiainphoto.ru/Ivan Shagin/MAMM/MDF)

friendly forces, setting up ambushes, activating partisan groups and executing prisoners of war, the Hungarians also became brutalized.

LESSONS LEARNT: HUNGARIAN

Hungarian involvement during the first phase of the war against the Soviet Union was minimal: just 89,505 men organized into five brigades and supporting troops. It should be remembered, though, that the Hungarians committed their most modern, partially motorized units, and deployed about 80 per cent of their armoured vehicles, motorized artillery troops and motor vehicles. Hungarian casualty rates were quite moderate compared to those of their allies and opponents, surprising even the Hungarian General Staff. During the four-month-long operation (30 July–30 November) the Mobile Corps suffered 4,420 casualties (9.94 per cent); while 12.86 per cent of officers became casualties, the rate among the other ranks was 9.83 per cent. The Hungarians lost 885 men killed or missing in action, 277 taken prisoner of war, 2,288 wounded and nearly 1,000 sick. These casualties were concentrated in the motorized rifle, light-tank and reconnaissance battalions, which lost half or more of their strength, while the cavalry, bicycle troops and artillery lost fewer men. The matériel losses were significant: the armoured units of the Mobile Corps lost all of their tankettes, 90 per cent of the 39M Csaba armoured cars and 80 per cent of the 38M Toldi light tanks (although the knocked-out or damaged armoured cars and light tanks were subsequently collected and transported back to Hungary for repair). The Hungarians also lost 28 artillery pieces, 21 aircraft and 1,200 trucks.

Excepting the Yugoslavian Campaign, which had lasted less than a week for the Hungarians, *Barbarossa* was the Royal Hungarian Army's first real combat operation. With no previous experience of operating mobile, mechanized forces in combat, the Hungarian commanders and troops had to learn 'the hard way' how to advance, reconnoitre and fight. During the first phase of the operation reconnaissance was neglected, and the Hungarian troops mounted headlong attacks against superior Soviet forces, which led to unnecessary casualties. Generally speaking, the Hungarian junior officers showed strong leadership skills and courage; they were flexible and innovative in the face of difficult tactical situations for which they had not been trained and for which they had to improvise tactical methods within the abilities of their troops and equipment. The units with the least tactical expertise proved to be the light-tank battalions, which lacked the knowledge and experience to deploy their vehicles in combat effectively.

During the 1941 fighting the Hungarian used combined-arms combat groups which, contrary to the tactical manuals, advanced in parallel and lacked proper reserve forces. By mounting counter-attacks the Red Army units could exploit their local numerical superiority to halt the advancing Hungarian units. Such clashes could develop rapidly and unexpectedly; the front lines were blurred and permeable, without clear boundaries between units. Learning from their initial mistakes, the Hungarians increased the distance between their reconnaissance troops and the main advance-guard units, thereby limiting the Soviet forces' ability to infiltrate the Hungarian positions, and deployed light howitzers and Bofors autocannon firing high-

explosive shells to eliminate the counter-attacking Red Army units. One field innovation was to deploy covert patrols in civilian clothing ahead of the Hungarian main body. Composed of troops with knowledge of Slavic languages, these patrols moved on foot or bicycle pretending to be lost Soviet soldiers and collecting information on the enemy and the local population.

Hungarian motorized riflemen armed with 35M rifles man a guard post covering their troops in the field. In the centre of the team is a corporal. (Fortepan/Kókány Jenő)

The 1941 battles made it clear that in general the Hungarian units had less firepower than their Soviet counterparts. The Hungarians had no submachine guns, their machine guns were elderly World War I models and fewer mortars were fielded than their opponents. The Hungarian anti-tank guns and anti-tank rifles, as well as the turret weapons of their armoured cars and light tanks, were only effective against the Soviet T-26 and BT light tanks. Although the Hungarian artillery, an elite branch of the Army, was considered to have performed well during the campaign, the brigade-level artillery batteries of the Mobile Corps were mostly distributed among the combat groups, leaving minimal artillery assets at the brigade commanders' disposal to deliver concentrated fire strikes. The rapid-firing 40mm Bofors anti-aircraft autocannon proved their worth as multi-functional weapons attached to the combat groups.

Although the domestically produced 38M Botond all-terrain squad-carrier trucks were among the best contemporary designs, the number of trucks, tractors and motorcycles was simply insufficient and the Mobile Corps had to rely on mobilized civilian vehicles, these requisitioned vehicles being concentrated in the supply echelons. In response, the Hungarians strove to upgrade their vehicle maintenance and recovery capacity at every level, and if possible to exclude the mobilized civilian vehicles from the motor pool of the motorized troops. The armoured vehicles of the Mobile Corps proved to be severely lacking in combat: the 35M tankettes were totally outdated, while the light armour and armament of the 38M Toldi light tanks and 39M Csaba

armoured cars meant they were suitable for the reconnaissance and liaison roles only. The lack of medium tanks and self-propelled anti-tank and anti-aircraft guns was a serious deficiency.

Logistics proved very difficult; the lines of communications were long and vulnerable, and the complexities of coalition warfare meant that the Hungarians had to use German supply centres located far behind the operational area, with the Hungarians being responsible for delivering the goods to the troops. It became evident during the campaign that the Hungarian planners had overestimated the consumption of small-arms ammunition and underestimated the rate at which infantry heavy weapons and artillery would consume ammunition. While captured Soviet supplies stocks eased the critical logistic shortfall somewhat, fuel shortages were a constant problem and hampered the operations of the Mobile Corps.

In the wake of the *Barbarossa* fighting the Hungarian mobile troops were reorganized: the motorized and cavalry/bicycle troops were separated from each other, the Mobile Corps was disbanded and a new I Armoured Corps with two armoured divisions and the 1st Cavalry Division was organized at the end of 1941. Most of the bicycle battalions were converted into tank battalions. The troops requested more automatic weapons, mortars and anti-tank guns, along with self-propelled anti-tank and anti-aircraft vehicles, medium tanks and assault artillery, in order to reach parity with their Soviet opponents. The firepower of the motorized rifle companies was supplemented with submachine guns for squad, platoon and company commanders in 1942; the motorized rifle battalions were each allocated an anti-tank company with six guns. The tankettes were removed from service and the 38M Toldi light tanks were allocated to the reconnaissance platoons of the tank companies and battalions. The manufacture of domestically produced armoured vehicles, Turán medium and heavy tanks, Nimród self-propelled anti-tank/anti-aircraft vehicles and 38M Botond trucks was accelerated to meet operational requirements. In 1942 the Germans handed over armoured vehicles sufficient for two tank battalions. From late 1941 onwards the new tactical and organizational changes were addressed during Hungarian officer training as well as during the troop exercises, incorporating the latest German tactical practices.

Aftermath

When the Mobile Corps ceased its operations and prepared to return to Hungary, the extraordinary territorial gains made by the Axis forces during Operation *Barbarossa* had not won the war for Hitler and his allies. In the face of determined Soviet resistance amid deteriorating weather conditions the pace of the Blitzkrieg slowed, the uncertainty of the situation compounded by the overstretched Axis supply system and the unexpected but highly effective effort made by the Red Army to replace its losses. Colonel Zsedényi, the chief-of-staff of the Mobile Corps, recalled how doubt set in among the Hungarians. The presence of huge maps of the Soviet Union in the public buildings in which he and his staff were quartered during the advance spurred Lieutenant-Colonel Ferenc Koszorús to measure the Hungarian advance on the map; the paltry distance travelled in relation to the vastness of the country prompted conflicting emotions in Zsedényi and his colleagues (Bokor 1982: 53).

The onset of the autumn rainy season hampered both sides' operations. Here, troops of the 1st Motorized Rifle Brigade are stuck in the mud near the River Donets in late October 1941. The 39M Csaba armoured car at right belongs to the 1st Reconnaissance Battalion; a Ford Marmon truck towing an ex-Polish fuel trailer, a local *panje* wagon and a 38M Botond truck are also visible. (Author's collection)

Official welcoming ceremonies were held at the garrisons for the returning troops of the Mobile Corps, the lessons of the campaign were identified and organizational and structural changes were implemented. Most of the Hungarian commanding officers were decorated and several were promoted. Lieutenant-General Szombathelyi became the Army chief-of-staff in September 1941, holding this position until April 1944; an advocate of Hungary's minimal military participation on the Eastern Front, he was executed as a war criminal by the Yugoslavians in November 1946. Major-Generál Miklós subsequently commanded II Corps and the 1st Hungarian Army; he took part in the ill-fated change-over to the Soviet side and in December 1944 became the first pro-allied prime minister of Hungary, dying in November 1948. Major-General Major was appointed to command the newly organized I Armoured Corps. Major-General Vörös, considered to be pro-German, served in different staff positions before being appointed Army chief-of-staff in spring 1944. Major-General Vattay commanded the 1st Cavalry Division and later II Replacement Corps in Poland, cooperating with Polish guerrillas in 1944.

The fiasco of the battle for Khortytsia did not rock the military career of Colonel Benda; he was promoted to major-general in 1944 and entered US captivity at the end of the war. After recovering from his wounds Captain Kárpáthy commanded a company of PzKpfw IV Ausf F1 medium tanks and later the II Battalion, 30th Tank Regiment (1st Armoured Field Division) at the River Don in 1942; wounded again, he returned to Hungary to assist in the organization of the newly created 2nd Armoured Division. The battalion commanders of the 1st Motorized Rifle Brigade led their units into battle again in 1942–43 at the River Don with the 1st Armoured Field Division.

Among the Soviet commanding officers of the 12th and 6th armies, six of them were captured with two dying in captivity, and three survivors were executed by the Soviets after the war. Captured in August 1941, Lieutenant-General Muzychenko survived to be cleared by the Soviet authorities in 1945. Major-General Galanin was promoted to lieutenant-general in January 1943 and went on to command the 4th Guards Army, retiring in 1946. Captured at Uman in August 1941, Major-General Kirillov and Major-General Ponedelin

spent almost four years in prison camps; having been blamed by Stalin for the disaster, they were condemned to death *in absentia*. After they were freed by US troops they were immediately arrested by Soviet counter-intelligence agents, falsely accused of cooperating with the Germans and eventually executed in August 1950. Both men were rehabilitated in 1956. Major-General Privalov, who went on to command the 15th Rifle Corps in 1942, was ambushed, wounded and captured by the Germans in December 1942. Also subsequently arrested by the Soviet authorities and falsely accused of cooperation with the enemy, Privalov was executed in December 1951, only to be rehabilitated in 1968. Captured at Uman, Major-General Proshkin died of typhus in January 1942. Colonel Shepetov was promoted to major-general in October 1941; he was made a Hero of the Soviet Union and commanded the 14th Guards Rifle Division before being captured in May 1942, and died in captivity in May 1943.

Major-General Markis B. Salikhov, who commanded the 60th Mountain Rifle Division, also belonging to the 12th Army, was a true traitor. In July 1941 he was sentenced to ten years' imprisonment – a sentence subsequently altered to demotion – and was captured by the Germans in August 1941. During Soviet interrogation in 1942 a captured German intelligence agent named Kopylov testified that one of his teachers at the German Intelligence School in Warsaw was Salikhov, using the pseudonym Osmanov; other captured German agents confessed and also identified him. Salikhov was tried *in absentia* and sentenced to death, but his subsequent fate is unclear (Maslov 2001: 305).

The Soviet soldiers who faced the Hungarian troops in 1941 shared the fate of the Soviet armed forces during Operation *Barbarossa*; those survivors still with their units endured horrendous personal traumas and matériel losses and continued the fight. Large numbers of their colleagues were captured by the advancing Hungarian troops; they were disarmed and interrogated, but were held only briefly by the Hungarians before being passed on to the German rear-area troops. Besides the captured soldiers, huge numbers of male civilians of military-service age were arrested and handed over to the German security units; captured armed civilians and suspected NKVD agents were summarily executed.

ABOVE LEFT
Soviet reinforcements heading towards the front. This motorized supply column consists of GAZ-AA 4×2 1.5-ton trucks transporting artillery ammunition. On the railway can be seen an artillery unit equipped with 152mm M1937 (ML-20) gun-howitzers, STZ-3 tracked artillery tractors and ammunition trailers. (russiainphoto.ru/Arkady Shaikhet)

ABOVE RIGHT
A GAZ-AAA truck with a 7.62mm Tokarev 4M four-barrelled machine gun on an anti-aircraft mount protects Soviet governmental buildings during the winter of 1941. (russiainphoto.ru/Mikhail Grachev)

UNIT ORGANIZATIONS

Soviet

The backbone of the Red Army was provided by its rifle divisions: 196 existed in June 1941. Officially introduced on 5 April 1941, the M41 rifle division had a strength of 14,483 men, reduced on 24 July 1941 to 10,859. Each Soviet rifle division facing the Hungarians had an HQ, three rifle regiments and five, later two, artillery battalions, each with three batteries of four guns, plus reconnaissance, anti-aircraft, anti-tank, engineer, signals and medical battalions as well as supply and support troops. Each rifle regiment had an HQ and three rifle battalions plus anti-aircraft, infantry gun, anti-tank and mortar batteries and also reconnaissance, engineer and signals companies. Each rifle battalion had an HQ, three rifle companies, a machine-gun company (12 Maxim M1910 medium machine guns) and a mortar company (six 82mm mortars), plus an anti-tank platoon (two 45mm anti-tank guns). Each rifle company had an HQ, a machine-gun platoon (two Maxim M1910 medium machine guns) and three rifle platoons, each with an HQ section and four 12-man rifle squads.

Officially fielding 13,369 men (the 60th Mountain Rifle Division had only 8,313), the M40 mountain-rifle division consisted of an HQ, four mountain-rifle regiments and two artillery regiments, plus anti-tank, anti-aircraft, reconnaissance, engineer, signals and medical battalions. The mountain-rifle regiment had five mountain-rifle companies, omitting the intermediate battalion echelon, plus machine-gun (12 medium machine guns), mortar (12 82mm mortars), engineer and signals companies and a mountain-gun battery (four 76.2mm mountain guns transported on pack horses). Each mountain-rifle company had one medium-machine-gun platoon with three machine guns and pack horses. Each rifle squad had one light machine gun with a pack horse. The divisional artillery consisted of one mountain-artillery regiment with two battalions, each with one mortar (six 107mm mortars) and two mountain-gun batteries (each with four 76.2mm mountain guns), and one field-howitzer regiment with two battalions, each with three batteries (each with four

122mm howitzers). The division's anti-tank battalion had just eight 45mm anti-tank guns. The troops were equipped with horsed and mule supply columns, but did not receive specific mountain training like their Hungarian equivalents.

An M41 mechanized division (11,200 all ranks) had an HQ, reconnaissance, anti-aircraft, anti-tank and engineer battalions, one light-tank regiment (five battalions), one motorized artillery regiment (three battalions, two with four 76.2mm guns and eight 122mm howitzers each and one with 12 152mm howitzers) and two motor-rifle regiments. Each motor-rifle regiment had an HQ and three motor-rifle battalions plus motorized anti-aircraft, anti-tank (six 45mm anti-tank guns) and artillery (four 76.2mm howitzers) platoons. Each motor-rifle battalion had an HQ and five motor-rifle companies, plus machine-gun (12 medium machine guns) and mortar (six 82mm mortars) platoons.

An M40 tank division (11,343 all ranks) had an HQ, two tank regiments, one motor-rifle regiment and one motorized artillery regiment, plus reconnaissance, anti-aircraft, anti-tank, signals and engineer battalions. Each tank regiment had one heavy (31 KV-1 tanks, two T-26 radio tanks and three BA-20 armoured cars), two medium (each with 50 T-34 tanks and one BA-20 armoured car) and one flame tank (27 T-26 flame tanks and nine T-26 radio tanks) battalions. The motor-rifle regiment had an HQ and three motor-rifle battalions, each with an HQ, three motor-rifle companies, one machine-gun company (18 medium machine guns) and one mortar company (six 82mm mortars).

The M41 cavalry division (9,240 all ranks) had an HQ, four cavalry regiments, one armoured regiment and a horsed artillery regiment, plus signals, engineer, medical, chemical-warfare and supply companies. Each cavalry regiment had an HQ, five cavalry companies, one machine-gun company (20 medium machine guns) and one horsed artillery company (four 76mm guns), plus anti-tank (two 45mm guns), anti-aircraft, engineer, chemical-warfare, signals and support platoons.

Hungarian

A motorized rifle brigade (roughly 10,000 all ranks) had three motorized rifle battalions, one bicycle/light-tank battalion, one bicycle battalion, one reconnaissance battalion and one artillery battalion (four batteries, each with four 105mm howitzers), plus an anti-aircraft battery, sapper and signals companies and a motorized supply group.

A motorized rifle battalion consisted of an HQ, three motorized rifle companies and one heavy-weapons company, plus signals, sapper, anti-tank and maintenance platoons. A motorized rifle company had 12 8mm 31M Solothurn light machine guns, four with tripod mounting for the anti-aircraft role, plus two 20mm 36M Solothurn anti-tank rifles and two 50mm 39M light mortars transported on 38M Botond all-terrain trucks. The heavy-weapons company had 12 8mm 07/31M Schwarzlose medium machine guns and four 81mm 36M mortars. These heavy weapons were transported by Krupp-Protze half-squad carrier trucks and Krupp-Protze light artillery tractors. The anti-tank platoon was armed with four 37mm 36M anti-tank guns.

A bicycle/light-tank battalion consisted of the battalion headquarters (three 38M Toldi light tanks), the 1st and 2nd Bicycle companies and the 3rd and 4th Light Tank companies (each with 18 38M Toldi light tanks), plus sapper, signals and maintenance platoons.

A reconnaissance battalion had one armoured-car company (16 39M Csaba armoured cars), one motorized rifle company and one motorcycle company, plus anti-tank (four 37mm 36M anti-tank guns), signals, maintenance and sapper platoons.

The most complicated units of the Mobile Corps were the bicycle battalions. Each consisted of three bicycle companies (each with 12 31M light machine guns and two 36M anti-tank rifles) and one motorized heavy-weapons company (six 07/31M Schwarzlose medium machine guns and two 81mm 36M mortars), plus sapper, signals, maintenance, anti-tank (four 37mm 36M anti-tank guns) and tankette (six FIAT Ansaldo tankettes) platoons. The bicycle battalion also had one motorized light field-howitzer battery, subordinated to the artillery battalion, equipped with four 105mm 37M howitzers and 37M Hansa-Lloyd half-tracked artillery tractors.

The 1st Cavalry Brigade (roughly 10,000 all ranks) had two hussar regiments, one armoured-cavalry battalion and two light-artillery battalions (one horsed and the other motorized), plus an anti-aircraft battery, signals and sapper companies and a mixed (horsed and motorized) supply group. The 1st Armoured Cavalry Battalion had one armoured-car company (16 39M Csaba armoured cars) and two tankette companies (totalling nine 38M Toldi light tanks and 36 35M FIAT Ansaldo tankettes).

These 38M Toldi light tanks of the 9th Bicycle/Light-Tank Battalion still bear the white Turul bird, the unit marking of the Light Tank Company of the 1st Armoured Cavalry Battalion. The 38M Toldi light tanks continued to form the backbone of the Hungarian armoured forces until mid-1942. (Zoltán Babucs)

BIBLIOGRAPHY

Andaházy-Szeghy, Viktor (2016). *A Magyar királyi honvédség részvétele a Szovjetunió elleni támadásban* [The participation of the Royal Hungarian Army in the operation against the Soviet Union]. Szeged: Belvedere.

Babucs, Zoltán (2006). *Jász vitézek Rajta, Előre* [History of the 9th Tank Battalion]. Nagykovácsi: Puedlo.

Becze, Csaba (2006). *Magyar Steel*. Petersfield: Mushroom Publications.

Bellamy, Chris (2007). *Absolute War: Soviet Russia in the Second World War*. London: Macmillan.

Bergström, Christer (2016). *Operation Barbarossa 1941: Hitler against Stalin*. Oxford: Casemate.

Bergström, Christer & Mikhailov, Andrey (2000). *Black Cross Red Star. The Air War over the Eastern Front, Volume I: Operation Barbarossa, 1941*. Pacifica, CA: Pacifica Military History.

Bernád, Dénes & Kliment, Charles K. (2015 & 2017). *Magyar Warriors: The history of the Royal Hungarian Armed Forces 1919–1945*. Two volumes. Warwick: Helion.

Bokor, László (1982). *Végjáték a Duna mentén* [End Game along the Danube]. Budapest: Minerva.

Carell, Paul (1991). *Operation Barbarossa in Photographs*. Atglen, PA: Schiffer Military History.

Cloutier, Patrick (2012). *Three Kings: Axis Royal Armies on the Russian Front 1941*. Milton Keynes: Lightning Source UK Ltd.

Drabkin, Artem (2010). *The Red Army at War*. Barnsley: Pen & Sword.

Dunnigan, James (1978). *The Russian Front: Germany's War in the East 1941–45*. London: Arms & Armour.

Glantz, David M. (1998). *Stumbling Colossus: The Red Army on the eve of World War*. Lawrence, KS: University Press of Kansas.

Glantz, David M. (2005). *Colossus Reborn: The Red Army at War, 1941–1943*. Lawrence, KS: University Press of Kansas.

Glantz, David M. (2011). *Operation Barbarossa: Hitler's Invasion of Russia 1941*. Stroud: The History Press.

Glantz, David M. & House, Jonathan M. (1995). *When Titans Clashed: How the Red Army Stopped Hitler*. Lawrence, KS: University Press of Kansas.

Haupt, Werner (1998). *Army Group South*. Atglen, PA: Schiffer Military History.

Irinarkhov, Ruslan (2012). *Neprostitelniy 1941. Chistoye porazhenie Krasnoy Armii* [Unforgivable 1941. The Pure Defeat of the Red Army]. Moscow: EKSMO.

Isaev, Aleksei (2017). *Dubno 1941, the Greatest Tank Battle of the Second World War*. Warwick: Helion.

Kamenir, Victor J. (2008). *The Bloody Triangle: The Defeat of the Soviet Armour in the Ukraine, June 1941*. Minneapolis, MN: Zenith Press.

Kershaw, Robert (2000). *War Without Garlands: Operation Barbarossa 1941/42*. London: Ian Allan.

Kirchubel, Robert (2003). *Operation Barbarossa (1): Army Group South*. Campaign 129. Oxford: Osprey.

Krivosheev, Grigori (1997). *Soviet Casualties and Combat Losses in the Twentieth Century*. London: Greenhill Books.

Martinez, Eduardo Manuel Gil (2019). *Hungarian Armoured Fighting Vehicles in the Second World War*. Barnsley: Pen & Sword.

Maslov, Aleksander A. (1998). *Fallen Soviet Generals: Soviet General Officers Killed in Battle 1941–1945*. Portland, OR: Frank Cass.

Maslov, Aleksander A. (2001). *Captured Soviet Generals: The Fate of Soviet Generals Captured by the Germans 1941–1945*. Portland, OR: Frank Cass.

Mujzer, Péter (2000). *Hungarian Mobile Forces 1920–45*. Bayside: Axis Europa Books.

Mujzer, Péter (2015). *Huns on Wheels: Hungarian Mobile Forces 1920–1945*. Budapest: Privately published.

Mujzer, Péter (2017). *Hungarian Armoured Forces in WW2*. Lublin: KAGERO Publishing.

Mujzer, Péter (2018). *Operational History of the Hungarian Armoured Troops in WW2*. Lublin: KAGERO Publishing.

Müller, Rolf-Dieter & Ueberschär, Gerd R. (1997). *Hitler's War in the East, 1941–1945: A Critical Assessment*. Oxford: Berghahn Books.

Niehorster, Leo (1998). *The Royal Hungarian Army 1920–45*. Bayside: Axis Europa Books.

Nuzhdin, Oleg (2015). *Umanskii Kotel. Tragediya 6-y i 12-y armiy* [Uman Kessel. The Tragedy of the 6th and 12th Armies]. Moscow: EKSMO.

Olive, Michael & Edwards, Robert (2012). *Operation Barbarossa and the Eastern Front 1941*. Barnsley: Pen & Sword.

Pleshakov, Constantin (2005). *Stalin's Folly: The Secret History of the German Invasion of Russia, June 1941*. London: Weidenfeld & Nicolson.

Rottman, Gordon L. (2007). *Soviet Rifleman 1941–45*. Warrior 123. Oxford: Osprey.

Runov, Valentin (2010). *1941. Pobedniy parad Gitlera: Pravda ob Umanskom poboishche* [1941. Hitler's Victory: The Truth about the Battle in Uman]. Moscow: EKSMO.

Saáry, Gábor Levente (2019). *A magyar gépkocsizó gyalogság létrejötte és szerepe az 1941. évi Szovjetunió elleni hadműveletekben* [Creation and role of the Hungarian motorized infantry during the operation of 1941]. Pécs: MOSZT.

Sárhidai, Gyula, Punka, György & Kozlik, Viktor (1996). *Hungarian Eagles: The Hungarian Air Forces 1920–1945*. Aldershot: Hikoki Publications.

Stephan, Robert W. (2004). *Stalin's Secret War: Soviet Counterintelligence against the Nazis, 1941–1945*. Lawrence, KS: University Press of Kansas.

Thomas, Nigel (2010). *World War II Soviet Armed Forces (1): 1939-41*. Men-at-Arms 464. Oxford: Osprey.

Thomas, Nigel & Szabó, László Pál (2008). *The Royal Hungarian Army in World War II*. Men-at-Arms 449. Oxford: Osprey.

Tucker-Jones, Anthony (2011). *Armoured Warfare on the Eastern Front*. Barnsley: Pen & Sword.

Tucker-Jones, Anthony (2013). *Armoured Warfare and Hitler's Allies 1941–1945*. Barnsley: Pen & Sword.

US War Department (1944). *Order of Battle and Handbook of the Hungarian Armed Forces*. Washington, DC: Military Intelligence Division.

Várhalmi, Iván (2012). *A Kárpát csoport majd az I. gyorshadtest hadműveletei a Szovjetunióban 1941.-ben* [Operations of the Carpathian Group and the I. Mobile Corps in Soviet Union, 1941]. Budapest: Privately published.

Various (2002). *Slaughterhouse: The Encyclopaedia of the Eastern Front*. New York, NY: The Military Book Club.

Zaloga, Steven J. (1989). *The Red Army of the Great Patriotic War 1941–45*. Men-at-Arms 216. Oxford: Osprey.

Zaloga, Steven J. (2013). *Tanks of Hitler's Eastern Allies 1941–45*. New Vanguard 199. Oxford: Osprey.

Zaloga, Steven J. & Grandsen, James (1983). *The Eastern Front*. London: Arms & Armour.

Zaloga, Steven J. & Ness, Leland S. (1998). *The Red Army Handbook 1939–1945*. Stroud: Sutton Publishing.

These three Soviet soldiers, from left a sub-lieutenant, a private and a senior sergeant, wear the *pilotka* cap and the M35 tunic; two of them have the double-lens goggles used by Red Army tank units. (Philippe Rio)

INDEX